Sharon,
Gordon Tender

Sex
Nutrition
and
You

By Gordon S. Tessler, Ph.D.

Editor: Gideon Thompson and DeJohna Vonson
Contributing Editor: Lynn Kay
Illustrators: Julie Lohnes and Pamela Beets
Cover Photography: D.J. Hawkins
Cover Model: Shauntelle LaRue

Published by Better Health Publishers

For information contact:

Better Health Publishers
3368 Governor Drive
Suite F-224
San Diego, CA 92122

ISBN: 0-932213-61-8
Printed in the United States of America

Second Printing

Dedication

This book is dedicated to all the wise people who are always willing to change their lifestyle in order to lead a healthier and happier life.

Acknowledgments

My heartfelt appreciation and everlasting gratitude to DeVona, president of Better Health Publishers, for her invaluable and untiring love and support of my work in the field of nutrition.

A special thanks to Bill Beitscher and other members of Better Health Publishers whose support made this book possible.

And finally, I wish to thank God from which all knowledge, understanding and wisdom comes. I thank Him for His Love and Truth which is my inspiration.

Table of Contents

Introduction

"We do not stop sexual activity because we grow old. We grow old because we stop sexual activity."
—Dr. Bernard Jensen

Most of the sexual books in print deal with the psychological, emotional and moral aspects of sex, but few explain the **nutrition of sex.** *Sex, Nutrition and You* is a book about the important interrelationship between optimum health and good sex.

Throughout human history there have never been two more indulged in bodily functions than sex and eating. The secret pleasures of each have pre-occupied man's mind, as well as his body, right up to the moment I am writing this book.

Both sex and food are necessary for the survival of humankind. Without food, we would die, and without sexual activity, we would become extinct. Both are considered by experts as basic desires or urges of our specie. We even intertwine the two in our language when we say, "sexual appetite." It is difficult to know where hunger ends and sexual appetite begins.

People are interested, curious, fearful, and perplexed about their sexuality. Sex is exploited in soap operas, movies, books, magazines, and at the spa. Yet with all the box office and press concerning sex, food is equally exciting, exotic and romantic. In fact, a person can go much longer without sex than without food! Next to the Bible, cookbooks are the most sought after books in print.

Scientific research has implicated the Standard American Diet (S.A.D.) of high protein and fat, excess salt and refined sugars, processed foods depleted in essential vitamins and minerals, and low in fiber, as a major culprit in the development of degenerative diseases. **The same poor nutrition that contributes to the development of heart disease and cancer is also involved in the increasing number of sexual disorders like impotency, frigidity, male and female infertility, miscarriages, pre-menstrual syndrome, menopausal distress and osteoporosis, hormonal imbalances, prostate troubles, and lack of sex drive.**

The following statistics related to sexual problems and dysfunctions have prompted the writing of this book:

1. In the U.S., the sperm count of the average adult male has declined to almost half since 1929.
2. Forty percent of menstruating women have symptoms of pre-menstrual syndrome (PMS).
3. One out of every ten men in the United States suffers from a chronic impotence.
4. Four of every seven men in the United States suffers from prostate problems.
5. Half of all married couples with wives in childbearing ages are sterile or have a childbearing impairment (infertility).
6. There are 400,000 miscarriages a year in the United States.
7. There are 250,000 children born a year with birth defects.
8. There are 90,000 new cases of prostate cancer a year in the U.S., 26,000 die.
9. There are 123,000 new cases of breast cancer a year, 40,000 die.
10. There are 33,000 new cases of ovarian and uterine cancer a year, 18,400 die.
11. There are 36,000 new cases of cervical cancer, 2,900 die.

12. There are 25,000 new cases of pancreatic cancer, 24,000 die.

Although sex is a natural experience, the knowledge of how to enhance your sex life does not come naturally. We often take sex for granted, asking our sexual organs to **deliver on demand,** while forgetting that they are part of the whole body. **The whole body must be in good health to sustain the activity of sex.** If your body is not receiving the nutritional support it requires to maintain the vital organ functions of the heart, kidneys, lungs, and liver, it will borrow the needed nutrients from the non-life-threatening organs (sexual organs). The sexual organs are expendable since we can live without them, i.e., hysterectomies, tubal ligations, and vasectomies are common surgical procedures today. **The malfunction of the sexual organs is an important indication of nutritional bankruptcy in other organs of your body.**

Nutritional imbalances and deficiencies affect every aspect of man's physical and mental life. **The function of all glands and organs is dependent upon proper nutrition and man's sex glands are no exception to the rule. An improved nutritional lifestyle in itself, will not guarantee sexual contentment, but it will improve sexual desire, performance and frequency.**

In the author's many years of nutritional counseling, the number one complaint of my clients was, **"I don't have any energy!"** Tiredness, fatigue and exhaustion are the most common symptoms. **A lack of energy and a lack of sex drive go hand in hand.** A healthy person has a healthy sex drive and sexual activity continues throughout a healthy person's life.

We are all products of sexual activity and equipped to have sex. **Your sexual health and your general health are one and the same.** Healthy sex and healthy sex drive are so fundamental to a well-balanced life that it is worth the effort to learn how to cultivate it. **When we understand the various factors that contribute to or undermine our sexual well-being, then we can take charge of and be charged by our sexual life.**

Sex is good for you, and you must be in good health to enjoy it fully. *Sex, Nutrition and You* will give you the knowledge you need to improve your health so that your organs will respond in the precise way you want them to. The foods, vitamins, minerals, aphrodisiacs, and natural hormones suggested in this book will help you maintain, as well as correct, sexual function. If you give your sexual organs the nutrition they need, they will do the rest.

Gordon S. Tessler, Ph.D.

"It is generally considered that the strength of the endocrine glands and particularly the sex glands, and their ability to produce sufficient hormones, is directly related to the general vitality and healthy functioning of the body. Sexual virility largely determines a man's youthfulness, health, vitality, and longevity. Likewise, plentiful sex hormone production in the female makes her look, feel, and act young. The decline in sex hormone production results in gradual aging and decreased life span." (Dr. Paavo Airola)

4

1

Endocrine Glands: The Spark Plugs of Your Sex Life

"We are as young as our glands."
—Dr. Bernard Jensen

Glands are small organs within your body that produce secretions which are either carried through a system of ducts or poured directly into the blood or lymph system. These tiny, yet vitally important glands perform thousands of functions a day, including regulating the temperature of the body, lubricating mucous membranes, controlling appetite, manufacturing sebum for the healthy growth of hair, enzymes for the proper digestion of carbohydrates, fats and proteins, and regulating the blood sugar. They produce tears, sweat, milk, seminal fluid, sperm, and hormones. The glands in your body number in the thousands and vary in size from microscopic to the size of the liver (several ounces), the largest gland in the body. Glands virtually control your physical, mental, emotional and sexual health.

The glands controlling the sexual function of your body are called *endocrine glands*. The endocrine glands are ductless structures whose chemical secretions known as hormones are released directly into the blood. The endocrine glands include the pituitary, hypothalamus, pineal, thyroid, parathyroid, thymus, adrenals, pancreas, ovaries, and testes.

The Endocrine System

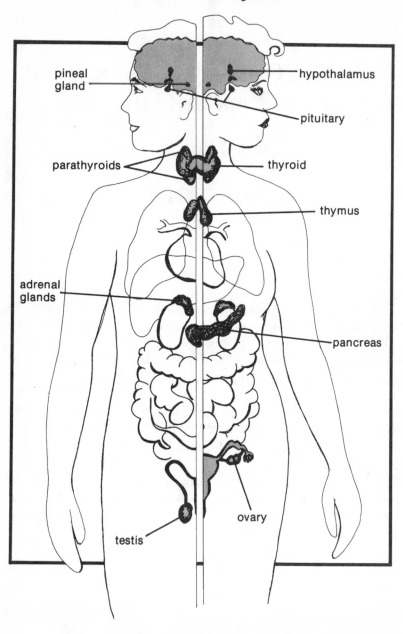

The hormones produced by these glands carry chemical messages or telegrams that communicate the changing needs of the body. Hormones, or specialized chemicals, circulating in the blood, travel various distances in order to monitor, regulate and stimulate various tissues and organs throughout the body. Each gland is a detector system able to evaluate a condition that needs regulation, and **each hormone is a messenger to stimulate an organ or tissue to take appropriate action.** The endocrine system is a very impressive glandular group that not only regulates all the physiological processes, but also helps determine whether you are emotionally stable, energetic, and agreeable, or depressed, tired, and critical. **These glands have a profound influence on your personality.**

Besides controlling the way you feel, the magic power of these glands also influence the way you look. **Early appearance of wrinkled skin, loss and greying of hair, loose and flabby skin, double chin, and protruding stomach and waistline are all signs of premature aging of the endocrine glands.**

Before we discuss how these neglected and malnourished glands can be fed in order to keep them young and vital, an explanation of what these glands are and how they work is important.

THE PITUITARY

This gland is about the size of a pea and is located at the base of the brain (see diagram). Even though the pituitary gland is quite small, it manufactures **nine hormones** that control the action of all the other endocrine glands. The pituitary gland has been called the **master gland**, because of the extensive roles it performs controlling and stimulating other glands.

This gland is divided into two parts: the anterior pituitary and the posterior pituitary. The anterior pituitary manufactures a growth hormone (GH) that regulates the growth of all tissues and bones. The under-secretion of this hormone results in dwarfism, while the over-secretion results in "giantism." Both conditions are effects of a defective pituitary. Other hormones produced by the anterior pituitary are melanocyte hormone (MSH), thyrotrophic hormone (TSH), adrenocorticotrophic hormone (ACTH), follicle stimulating hormone (FSH), leutenizing hormone (LH), and prolactin (LTH). TSH stimulates the functioning of the thyroid and helps to control the storage and distribution of fat. (Gross obesity can be a result of pituitary imbalances.) ACTH stimulates the adrenal cortex, and the inadequate function of this hormone makes a person sensitive to colds, infections, and generally lowers resistance under stress.

FSH stimulates growth of ovaries in women and testes in men. LH regulates the secretion of sex hormones by ovaries and testes. These two specific gonadotrophic hormones act directly to stimulate the sexual organs (gonads) of men and women. LTH stimulates milk secretion by mammary glands of the breast. The posterior pituitary serves as a storage organ for the hormones, oxytocin and vasopressin, both of which are produced by the hypothalamus.

The malfunction of the pituitary retards production of sex hormones in both males and females. Under the direct stimulus of the pituitary, the ovaries produce ova (eggs) and the testes produce spermatozoa (sperm).

THE HYPOTHALAMUS

This gland is structurally linked to the pituitary and produces two important hormones: oxytocin, a hormone that stimulates contraction of the uterine muscles, and vasoprossin, which regulates the metabolism of water and salts by the kidneys and constriction of blood vessels (blood pressure). **Malfunction of this vital gland can cause an imbalance of the pituitary sex hormones, as well as causing water retention and kidney problems.** The hypothalamus integrates the function of the endocrine and nervous systems. When your sense organs detect a sexual stimulus, this impulse is transmitted from the nervous system to the

8

hypothalamus. The hypothalamus stimulates the anterior pituitary to secrete gonadotrophic hormones that in turn stimulate the gonads to secrete more sex hormones.

The main control of hormonal secretions of the hypothalamus is based on a "feedback" system from the hormones in the blood and impulses from the nervous system. This form of control allows the human body to cope with the normal stresses and sexual stimulations of life in a smooth and coordinated fashion.

THE PINEAL

The functions of this gland are still not clearly defined or understood. Sunlight enters the eyes and triggers nerve impulses which stimulate the pineal. The nerve impulses are fed from the pineal to the hypothalamus and pituitary, which control vital sex functions and sex hormone production.

Melatonin, a hormone produced by the pineal when stimulated by light, may help sexual function by regulating the pituitary, adrenals, ovaries, and tests. Melatonin can stop the ovaries from ovulating. It also appears to be involved in the regulation of ovary and teste development. When melatonin is given to patients it induces sleep and will actually change the brain wave pattern on an electroencephalogram. Melatonin works in the brain to regulate the sleep/wake cycles. The pineal gland is called "the peace gland," because of its biochemical effect in rest and relaxation.

THE THYROID

The thyroid gland is located at the base of the neck. It consists of two lobes full of follicles containing iodine. The thyroid, dependent upon the hormones of the pituitary, produces thyroxin (T_4), which activates the oxygen metabolism of all the cells of the body. The thyroid affects hair growth and texture, nail growth, and complexion. **An underactive thyroid contributes to diminished sex drive and sexual capacity, sluggish metabolism and resultant obesity, chronic** fatigue, irregular and/or excessive menstruation, headaches, inability to concentrate, crying spells and unjustified fears and worry. Another thyroid hormone, **triiodothyromine** (T_3) performs duties similar to that of thyroxin, only it is three to five times more active and is secreted in smaller amounts. **Calcitonin**, another thyroid hormone, prevents excessive calcium accumulation in the blood and acts to stop withdrawal of calcium from the bones. Calcitonin also slows the absorption of calcium from the intestines during digestion. **The thyroid plays a key role in your sexual life. A lazy thyroid can cause both men and women to lose interest in sex.**

THE PARATHYROID

The parathyroid glands are four small pea-like organs, located on the surface of the thyroid. Even though they are connected to the thyroid, their functions are totally separate from it. They secrete a hormone called **parathormone**, which regulates the calcium and phosphorous supply to the blood and body tissues.

This gland can increase the amount of calcium in the blood by stimulating its release from the bones and at the same time inhibiting the excretion of calcium by the kidneys and intestines. Any decrease in calcium levels contribute to menstrual irregularities and cramps, osteoporosis, estrogen depletion, and irritability.

If the parathyroid becomes overactive by being enlarged or developing tumors, excessive calcium is withdrawn from the bones. The over-stimulated parathyroids draw calcium from the bones, upsetting estrogen levels in the blood. The bones can then become weak and brittle, resulting in a condition called osteoporosis.

An imbalance in this gland can cause an increase in phosphorus and decrease in calcium in the blood which can in turn produce serious disturbances in the function of **muscles** like the penis and vagina and even convulsions.

THE THYMUS

Like the thyroid, the thymus is a two-lobed gland. It is located below the thyroid and above the heart and plays an essential role in early growth. **It manufactures cells that help build immunity and therefore is involved in the defense against sexual infections and disease.** Thymosin, a hormone produced by the thymus, stimulates immunologic competence and raises resistance, particularly in the lymph tissues. The thymus provides the initial supply of functional lymphocytes for many immunological mechanisms of the body. For decades biologists could not assign a function to the thymus, and this gland was once considered useless since it nearly disappears in adulthood. Some researchers link early childhood innoculation to its shrinkage and diminished function. In the last few years, the thymus has been the subject of intensive research. **The findings establish the importance of the thymus in the development of your defense system against sexual and other diseases.**

THE PANCREAS

The pancreas, located near the stomach, is considered a digestive organ. The digestive enzymes, **amylase** (enzyme for digestion of starches), **lipase** (enzyme for digestion of fats), and **protase** (enzyme for digestion of proteins) secreted by the pancreas, are vital in the process of digestion and assimilation of food. In fact, the pancreas plays a larger role in digestion than does the stomach. It digests the carbohydrates so vital for sexual energy.

Insulin is a hormone that helps regulate the amount of sugar or glucose in the bloodstream. It stimulates the liver and the muscles to convert excess glucose into glycogen for storage in the liver and muscles. A lack of sufficient insulin production by the pancreas results in diabetes. Insulin also encourages amino acid incorporation into tissue protein.

Glucagon, the other pancreatic hormone, has the opposite effect of insulin; it causes an increase in blood-glucose concentration (raises blood sugar).

These pancreatic hormones—insulin and glucagon—are involved in carbohydrate metabolism, which is the important process of converting carbohydrates into glucose. Sexual vitality in part comes from adequate supplies of glucose. **The blood glucose level is very precisely regulated by these hormones since glucose is the only energy source that the brain is capable of utilizing.** This vital energy, glucose, helps stimulate the functioning of the hypothalamus, pineal, and pituitary glands, all vital to sexual activity.

THE ADRENALS

The two adrenal glands, as their name suggests (ad means at and renal refers to the kidney), are just above each kidney. Each adrenal is actually a double gland, constructed of an inner core, the **medulla**, and an outer skin called the **cortex**. The medulla and the cortex and their functions are unrelated.

The adrenal medulla secretes two hormones, **adrenalin** (also known as epinephrine) and **noradrenalin** (norepinephrine). Adrenalin, the fight or flight hormone, increases blood pressure, accelerates the heartbeat, increases conversion and release of glucose into the blood by the liver, increases blood flow to skeletal and heart muscles, and dilates the pupils. Both adrenalin and noradrenalin production is enhanced during times of stress, physical exertion (heavy exercise), heightened emotional states, and sexual activity. **Without the adrenals, sex would be very tiring.** These important hormones stimulate the body during times of emergency.

A person can live without the adrenal medulla (sympathetic nervous system stimulates the fight or flight reactions), but if the **adrenal cortex** is removed, death follows. They are vital to life perhaps because the adrenal cortex produces at least fifty different hormones, of which nine or ten are very active. **These cortical hormones are all steroids.** The over-production or administration of certain steroid hormones can result in decrease in production of sperm (sterility), and degeneration of the testicles in men and failure to menstruate in women.

The cortical hormones may be grouped into three categories on the basis of their function:

1. **Glucocorticoids**, which regulate carbohydrate and protein metabolism. Hormones in this category include corticosterone, cortisone, and hydrocortisone. Of these hormones, hydrocortisone is the most important, since it stimulates conversion of amino acids in the muscles.

2. **Mineralocortiroids**, which regulate salt and water balance. Hormones in this category include eldosterone and deoxycorticosterone, which stimulate the kidneys in the absorption of potassium and sodium, as well as increasing blood pressure. These important hormones, along with pituitary hormones, regulate the body's internal fluid environment.

3. **Sex hormones**, adrenosterone, androgens, and estrogens. Hormones in this category are similar to the sex hormones produced by the gonads. They stimulate male characteristics such as beard growth, lower voices, and maturing of the genital organs. Although there are both male and female cortical sex hormones, the male hormones predominate. If these cortical sex hormones are over-produced due to tumors of the adrenal cortex in a female, she will develop masculine characteristics such as a deeper voice, masculine musculature, and hair on the face and chest. The similarity between the sex hormones of the adrenal cortex and those of the gonads may stem from the development of these glands in the fetus. They begin their development in the embryo **side by side** in the same tissue.

THE GONADS (GENITALS)

The hormones of all endocrine glands (pituitary, hypothalamus, pineal, thymus, pancreas, and adrenals) have a direct or indirect influence on sexual drive and performance. The body is also equipped with specific glands which are directly involved in reproduction. These reproductive glands are called **gonads** generally and are further divided into testes in men and ovaries in women.

Reproduction is the central theme of life. Other aspects of living—digestion, circulation, excretion, fluid balance, growth, nervous system activities, and even behavior—are processes that enable humans to survive to reproduce. We are an elaborate organism for producing eggs and sperms for bringing them together for fertilization to assure the continuation of the human species. An old farmer's axiom is, "The hen is the egg's way of producing another egg!" This idea is true of man also.

THE OVARIES

The female gonads are called the **ovaries**, which are located in the lower part of the abdominal cavity and held in place by large ligaments. The ovaries consist of two small glands, each the size of an almond, situated on both sides of the uterus. The ovaries have two main functions: (1) Producing eggs and (2) secreting sex hormones.

At the time of birth, a female's ovaries **already** contain from 100,000 to 1,000,000 immature egg cells. Beginning of puberty and continuing during 30 or more years of her reproductive life, about thirteen times per year, only about 390 eggs ever mature and leave the ovaries forming one mature egg cell, or ovum, each time.

Approximately every 28 days a **follicle** filled with fluid surrounding the ripe ovum (egg) ripens, bulges from the surface of one ovary and breaks, sending fluid and ovum into one of the **fallopian tubes**. There is no apparent regularity as to which ovary will supply an egg at any given time. If sperm is present, the egg is fertilized while still in the upper third of the fallopian tube. If more than one ovum is released at a time, multiple births may occur. The fallopian tube empties the fertilized ovum into the upper end of the **uterus** (womb) where the embryo develops until the time of birth approximately nine months later. The uterus, which is located behind the bladder, is an organ with a mucus lining and muscular wall (one of the strongest muscles in the body) strong enough to hold a full grown infant. The uterus is influenced by numerous sex hormones from the endocrine glands and can be the source of many female problems. During the birth process, the infant passes through a muscular ring of tissue at the mouth of the uterus called the **cervix**, into another elastic muscular tube known as the **vagina** on its way out of the mother's body.

The vagina is the organ of sexual intercourse, as well as the birth canal. It acts as the receptacle for the male penis and its many folds increase friction, intensifying sensation during intercourse. The opening of the vagina in a young female is partially closed by a thin membrane called the **hymen**. Traditionally, the hymen is regarded as the symbol of virginity which is destroyed at the first time intercourse takes place.

The external opening of the female genitalia or **vulva** consists of two folds of skin or "lips" which surround the opening to the vagina. At the lower end of the vagina where the lips meet, is a small organ called the **clitoris**. The word clitoris means "key" in Greek. This organ is abundantly supplied with sensitive nerve endings that can be stimulated to enhance sexual excitement. The same embryonic tissue which forms the penis in a male, forms the clitoris in a female and it, like the penis, can become erect, increasing in size (up to an inch) when engorged with blood during sexual excitement.

Female Reproductive System

(Front view)

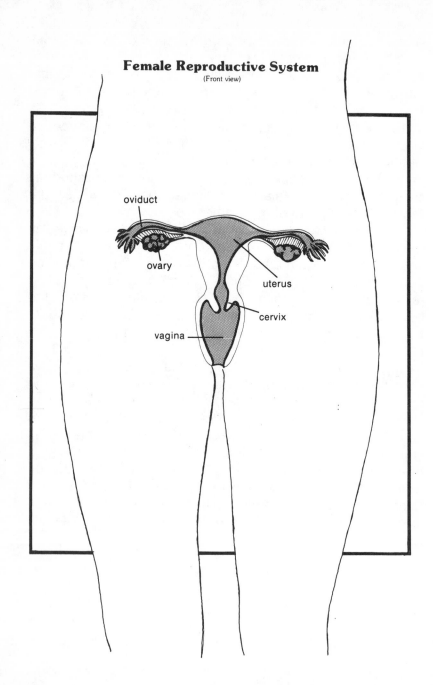

oviduct

ovary

uterus

cervix

vagina

Female Reproductive System

(Side view)

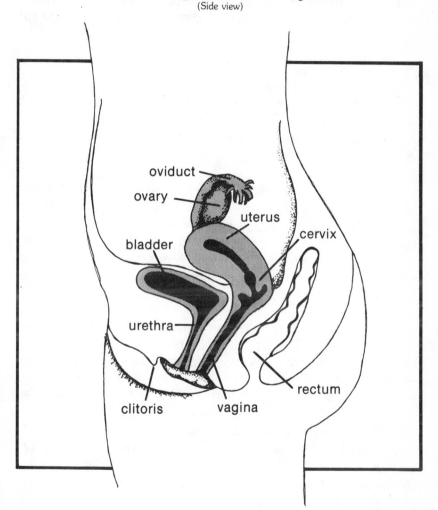

oviduct

ovary

uterus

bladder

cervix

urethra

clitoris

vagina

rectum

FEMALE SEX HORMONES

Puberty begins when the hypothalamus stimulates the anterior pituitary to secrete increased amount of FSH (follicle stimulating hormone) and LH (lutenizing hormone). These gonadotrophic hormones cause maturity of the ovaries, which then begin secreting the female sex hormones, **estrogen** and **progesterone**. These sex hormones, particularly estrogen, stimulate development of the female secondary sexual characteristics:

1. Growth of pubic hair
2. Broadening of the pelvis
3. Development of the breasts
4. Increase in size of the uterus and vagina
5. Change in voice quality
6. Onset of menstrual cycles

An estrogen deficiency in a mature woman may cause her complexion to appear flabby and wrinkled, making her appear years older than her actual age. Many scientists believe that aging is tied to the hormone production of the sex glands. Although the ovaries will eventually stop producing ova and sex hormone secretion will diminish or stop altogether, proper nutrition and supplementation can slow down the aging of the sex glands. The FSH of the anterior pituitary, after stimulation by the hypothalamus, stimulates the growth of follicles in the ovaries. The growing follicles then begin secreting the first of the two female hormones, estrogen. The increasing estrogen in the blood instructs the hypothalamus to store stimulating the pituitary to make FSH and at the same time increases the stimulation of the hypothalamus which results in the secretion of LH from the pituitary. The LH brings the follicle of the ovary to maturity, causes it to rupture, and ovulation begins. The ruptured follicle, under the influence of LH, is converted into a yellowish mass of cells called the **corpus luteum** (Latin for yellowish body). The corpus luteum continues secreting estrogen and a second female sex hormone, **progesterone.**

Progesterone is the hormone of pregnancy for it stimulates the complex system of glands in the lining of the uterus to receive the embryo. Progesterone also inhibits the production of FSH by the hypothalamus and pituitary. The restriction of FSH insures that a new cycle will not be triggered. Progesterone helps regulate the duration of the menstrual cycle. Birth-control pills, which contain synthetic compounds of progesterone and estrogen, inhibit both FSH and LH secretion and thus prevent follicle growth and ovulation. No ovulation, no conception.

THE TESTES (MALE)

The male sex organs are called the testes. Each testis is composed of two parts: (1) **Seminiferous tubules** in which sperm cells are produced; (2) **Interstitual cells** which secrete male sex hormones. The seminiferous tubules are not functional at temperatures as high as in the abdominal cavity and thus the testes descend in the **scrotal sac**, away from the body, where the temperature is approximately three degrees cooler. Tight pants or underwear push the scrotal sac nearer the warm body, killing vital sperm.

Mature sperm stored in the **epididymis**, a tube which lies on the surface of the testes, and are released during ejaculation. The sperm duct or tube (vasdeferns), runs from the epididymis into the abdominal cavity where it bypasses the **bladder** and joins with the urethra. The urethra passes through the **penis** and empties to the outside. The urethra is the common passage way used for both urine and semen.

As sperm travel through the vasdeferens and urethra, seminal fluid is added to the sperm calls to form **semen**. Seminal fluid is secreted by three sets of glands: (1) **Seminal vesticles**, which empty into the vasdeferens; (2) **Prostate**, which empties into the first part of the urethra; (3) **Cowper's glands**, emptying into the urethra at the base of the penis.

Seminal fluid performs four important functions:

1. Transports the sperm
2. Lubricates passages where sperm travels
3. Provides an alkaline medium to protect sperm from acid of female genitals
4. High in Sugar (mostly fructose) which the active sperm use as their main source of energy (food)

The prostate gland located below the bladder, produces the alkaline seminal fluid which combines with sperm. This gland can become inflamed or enlarged due to over-acid diet of meat, dairy and starch which is described in another chapter. The Cowper's glands produce the slippery fluid which lubricates the penis and the female sexual organs during intercourse.

The penis is the organ designed for sexual contact with the female. It becomes rigid (erect) in order to facilitate entry into the vagina. If a male is unable to achieve or sustain an erection, he is termed impotent. If insufficient sex hormones are manufactured, erection is impossible.

MALE SEX HORMONES

In males, the beginning of puberty is triggered by the increased release of anterior pituitary hormones in the testes. FSH stimulates the maturation of the seminiferous tubles (which produce sperm cells) and LH stimulates maturation of the interstitial cells (which secrete sex hormones). The hypothalamus, as in the female, stimulates the release of both FSH and LH by the pituitary.

The interstitial cells of the testes, stimulated by the LH produced by the pituitary, secrete the male sex hormone, **testosterone**. Testosterone produces the secondary sexual characteristics normally associated with puberty: Growth of beard, deepening of voice, development of the prostate, and development of larger and stronger muscles. Testosterone, besides being critical to the development of male characteristics, retards the aging process of men. Youthful virility, sexual potency and activity are dependent on the sex glands and their hormone producing potential.

Male Reproductive System
(Front view)

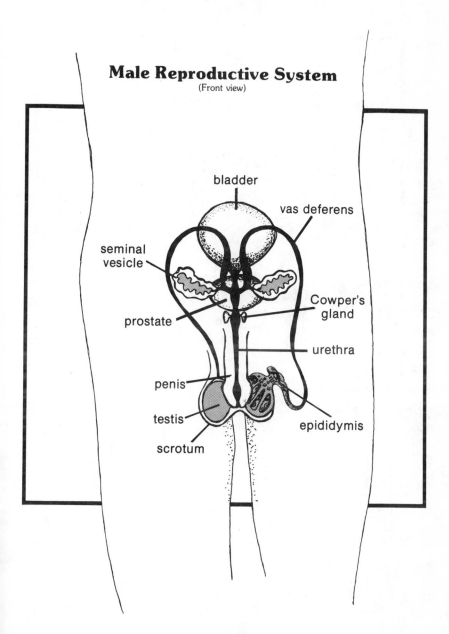

bladder

vas deferens

seminal
vesicle

Cowper's
gland

prostate

urethra

penis

testis

epididymis

scrotum

Male Reproductive System

(Side view)

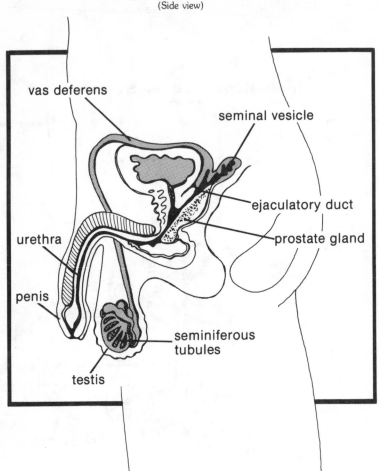

Hormones of the Endocrine Glands

GLANDS	HORMONE	FUNCTIONS

PITUITARY
• Anterior
	GH (Growth Hormone)
	TSH (Thyrotrophic Hormone)
	ACTH (Adrenocorticotropic Hormone)
	Gonadotrophic Hormones:
	   FSH (Follicle-stimulating Hormone)
	   LH (Lutenizing Hormone)
	LTH (Prolactin)
	MSH (Melanocyte)
		Stimulates growth
		Stimulates thyroid
		Stimulates adrenal cortex
		Stimulates growth of ovarian follicles and seminiferous
		  tubules of testes
		Stimulates secretion of sex hormones of ovaries and testes
		Stimulates milk secretion by mammary breast glands
		Controls skin pigmentation

• Posterior	Stores Oxytocin Vasopressin produced by hypothalmus	See Hypothalamus
HYPOTHALAMUS	Releasing Factors Oxytocin Vasopressin	Regulate hormone secretion by anterior pituitary and stimu- lates contraction of uterine muscles Stimulates release of milk by mammary glands Stimulates increased water reabsorption by kidneys and Stimulates constriction of blood vessels and smooth muscles
PINEAL	Melatonin	Regulates pituitary, perhaps by regulating hypothalamus
THYROID	Thyroxin (T4) Triidolhyronine (T3) Calcitonin	Stimulates oxidation metabolism Prevents excessive use in blood calcium
PARATHYROID	Parathromone	Regulates calcium-phosphorus metabolism
THYMUS	Thymosin	Stimulates immunological response
PANCREAS	Insulin Glucagon	Stimulates glycogen formation and storage and stimulates carbohydrate oxidation Stimulates conversion of glycogen to glucose

ADRENALS
• Medulla
 	
• Cortex
	Adrenalin (epinephrine)
	Noradrenalin (Norepinephine)
	
	Glucocorticoids/Corticosterone
	(Cortisone, hydrocortisone)
	Mineralocorticoids
	(Aldosterone deoxycorticosterone)
	Cortical sex hormones
	(Adrenosterone, androgens, estrogens)
		Stimulates reaction termed "fight or flight" part of the process
		  of glycogen into glucose conversion
		Stimulates reaction similar to those produced by adrenalin
		  (less effective)
		Inhibits incorporation of amino acids into protein in muscles
		  and stimulates formation and storage of glycogen
		Helps maintain normal blood-sugar level
		Regulates sodium-potassium balance
		Stimulate secondary sexual characteristics, particularly of the
		  male.

TESTES	Testosterone	Stimulates development and maintenance of male secondary sexual characteristics and behavior

OVARIES	Estrogen
	Progesterone
		Stimulates development and maintenance of female second-
		  ary sexual characteristics and behavior, and maintains
		  pregnancy

*Biological Science, William T. Keeton, Cornell University.

Hormone - Is an internal secretion of the endocrine glands, such as insulin, epinephrine, etc., carried by the blood to other organs, where it stimulates them to physiological activity.

CONCLUSION

The purpose of this chapter, which outlines the endocrine glandular system, is to impress upon you the vital importance of these glands. **The common belief that only the sex organs have something to do with sex hormones and sexual activity is inaccurate. All** the glands—pituitary, hypothalamus, pineal, thyroid, parathyroid, pancreas, and adrenals, as well as the testes and ovaries play direct or indirect roles in the production of sex hormones and the stimulation of sexual function in you body. Not only do they regulate all your sexual processes, they also enable you to digest and assimilate food into every living cell of energy needed for sexual activity. They also control, influence, and determine to some extent your personality and mental make-up.

Since all of these glands have a profound effect upon your life and personality, you should do all you can to insure their healthy functioning. **Research has found that the health of your glands is dependent to a large degree on your nutrition.** The proper function of these miracle workers, your glands, is sustained by feeding them all the vitamins, minerals, fatty acids, proteins, carbohydrates, enzymes, and natural hormones they need. **These nutrients can best be found in the foods you eat.** Selecting proper foods and balancing your nutrition will feed your glands. Proper nutrition for your glands promises greater vitality, trouble-free service and optimum health. No matter what your age, the information contained in *Sex, Nutrition and You*, will help you improve and maintain optimum sexual vitality and interest throughout your life.

2

Vitamins and Minerals: Feed Your Sex Glands

"Gold is valuable, Health is priceless."
—GST

SUPPLEMENTATION

There are those in the nutrition field who insist that food supplements are unnecessary. Food supplements consist of vitamins, minerals, and herbs (in pill, powder or liquid form) which are added to a diet to enhance the nutrient content of food. Those opposed to vitamin and mineral supplementation argue that if a diet is "well balanced," a person will obtain all the vitamins and minerals needed to maintain good health. Ideally, we should be able to eat a healthy diet and absorb all the protein, carbohydrates, fats, vitamins and minerals which our bodies need for optimum health. However, there are many factors that make this ideal impossible.

REASONS FOR TAKING SUPPLEMENTS ARE:

1. The poor quality of foods grown in depleted soil.
2. Modern refining and processing of foods.
3. Urban crowding which increases exposure to viruses and infections.
4. Mental and emotional stresses of urban living.
5. Constant exposure to air pollutants, chemicals and other carcinogenic substances in the environment.
6. Inherited vitamin and mineral deficiencies.

Nutritious foods are vital to your glands because of certain vitamins and minerals they contain. Following is a list of vitamins and minerals crucial to the optimum function of all your sex glands.

MINERALS

Without a proper mineral balance, our bodies cannot absorb or hold vitamins. Before vitamins, before man, the ancient earth was composed of inorganic minerals. Prehistoric plant life utilized and transformed these inorganic minerals, which animals could not assimilate, into useful organic forms.

As we study nature and life processes, we arrive at one inescapable conclusion: **the smaller the element, the more powerful its consequences.** Although minerals make up only a small percentage of our bodies, about five pounds, they determine to a large degree our state of health.

Minerals are divided into **major minerals** and **trace minerals**, depending upon whether a mineral is greater or lesser than five grams (a teaspoon). The distinction between major and trace minerals **does not** infer one group is more important than the other. Deficiencies of a few micrograms of iodine (a trace mineral) would cause serious thyroid problems as would a few micrograms of copper (a trace mineral) cause anemia.

Minerals harden our teeth and bones, assist digestion and hormone production, and help us utilize nutrients in the foods we eat. Without minerals we would be unable to maintain fluid balance, transport nutrients in cellular metabolism, produce antibodies to fight infection or reproduce.

HOW MINERALS AFFECT YOUR SEX LIFE

CALCIUM

Calcium represents the largest quantity (1150 grams, 2.5 pounds or half) of the major minerals found in the human body.

MINERALS IN A 60-KILOGRAM PERSON

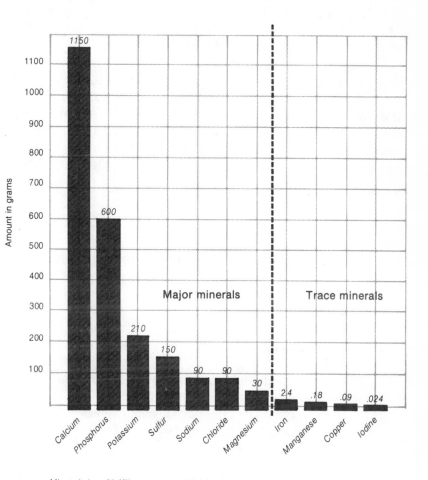

Minerals in a 60-Kilogram person (132 lbs.) (1 kilogram = 2.2 lbs.)
Source: Nutrition Concepts and Controversies (Hamilton and Whitney)

Calcium is important to practically all the sex glands of the body and is regulated by **parathormone**, a hormone of the parathyroid glands. A **decreased calcium level can cause painful menstrual cramps, irritability, and nervousness during periods, and a decrease of sex hormones, especially estrogen.** It works in combination with other glandular minerals and vitamins. Calcium needs to combine with magnesium, phosphorous, and/or vitamins A, C, and D for proper utilization. Hormones regulate calcium's absorption.

Calcium is essential to bone formation. But a less known fact about bones is that they are not solid like rocks. Bones are soft enough to both add calcium and remove calcium as the body demands change. The bones and the teeth act as reservoirs where calcium can be deposited or withdrawn. Approximately 99% of all the calcium in the body is found in the bones; the remaining one percent circulates throughout the body performing the following:

Roles of Calcium

1. Important in nerve transmission
2. Builds and maintains bones and teeth
3. Required for muscle contraction
4. Helps regulate the heartbeat
5. **Aids in iron utilization**
6. A catalyst for many metabolic functions
7. Assists in process of blood clotting
8. Helps maintain an alkaline balance in blood
9. **Helps regulate fluid or water balance in and out of cells**
10. Regulates nutrients in and out of cells
11. **Helps regulate sex hormones, especially estrogen**
12. Essential to thyroid function

Major Causes of Calcium Deficiency

1. **A high fat diet inhibits the absorption of calcium.** Excess fat binds the calcium into a soapy material which is excreted in the feces.

2. Excess ingestion of phosphorous promotes the excretion of calcium. As the body eliminates excess phosphorous, calcium will be removed along with it.
   a. A **high animal protein** diet, rich in phosphorous is particularly responsible for calcium loss. Such a diet is common among Americans.
   b. Also phosphate-containing drinks like regular and diet pop, contributes to calcium depletion.

3. **Refined sugar has had the calcium removed and consequently requires calcium to be taken from bones and teeth in order to digest this empty-caloried product.** According to statistics, most of us can expect to have some form of osteoporosis, or arthritis in our lifetime. Osteoporosis is the thinning of bones or removal of calcium from the bones. One of the leading causes of osteoporosis is the use of refined sugar, which forces the body to use up its own calcium and magnesium storage. As calcium and magnesium are removed from the bones, they end up in the soft tissues of the body, including the hair and the joints. This accumulation of calcium in the joints is commonly referred to as arthritis. Approximately 75% of men and women over 60 have some form of osteoporosis or arthritis. Is it old age which caused these degenerative conditions or the consumption of the thief called refined sugar?

4. Coffee, black tea, alcohol, prescription drugs and excessive stress are other major causes of calcium deficiencies.

5. A further concern is that some drugs such as antacids, steroids, and tetracycline can interfere with calcium utilization.

6. A lack of hydrochloric acid in the stomach or Vitamin C can decrease the solubility of calcium which lowers calcium absorbability.

Many Americans are operating on an **"overdraft"** with their calcium bank in the bones. The Standard American Diet (S.A.D.), containing 140 pounds of refined sugar a year, 50% of the daily calories as fat, two to three times the amount of protein (red meats—rich in excess phosphorous), coffee, diet sodas, alcohol, and stress is the cause that ends up plaguing many of us later in our lives.

Symptoms of Calcium Deficiencies

1. Osteoporosis
2. Arthritis
3. Muscle cramps
4. Nervous afflications
5. Numbness
6. Tingling in hands and feet
7. "Popping" or "Cracking" in bones
8. Swollen or aching joints
9. Headaches
10. Insomnia
11. Heart palpitations
12. Hypertension
13. **Low estrogen levels**
14. **Menstrual irregularities**
15. Tooth decay
16. Rickets
17. Stiffness
18. Burning in stomach

Food Sources of Calcium

Nuts and seeds — almonds, chia seeds, sesame seeds, brazil nuts, filberts

Whole grains — barley, beans, brown rice, buckwheat, millet, oats, rye, lentils, cornmeal (yellow)

Vegetables —	brussel sprouts, broccoli, cauliflower, parsnips, onions, green vegetables, avocados, carrots
Fish —	avoid shell fish; **fin** and **scale are best**
Egg —	yolks
Dairy —	yogurt
Sea vegetables —	kelp, dulse, agar-agar

Approximately 30% of ingested calcium is absorbed; the rest is excreted in the stool.

Poor Sources of Calcium

Dolomite is a rock and is not very usable by humans (potential lead toxicity).

Bone Meal — humans don't digest bones well (potential lead toxicity).

Although bone meal and dolomite are popular forms of calcium supplementation, they are the least advisable. According to Dr. Jacobs, Chief of Nutrient Toxicity at the Food and Drug Administration, extensive analysis of bone meal supplements reveal they contain at least six parts per million of **lead**. (Five ppm is upper limit for lead contamination in food products.) Because bones are **dumping ground** for toxic metals from circulation, bone meal is a dangerous source for calcium supplementation. Dolomite, a rock, is a form of carbonate which also contains lead and is not recommended.

Oyster Shell — shells do not assimilate well in humans.

Calcium Carbonate — nothing more than pure limestone, insoluable in water and very constipating.

Calcium Carbonate is the most popular form of calcium

supplementation because it is a very **cheap** source of calcium. Calcium Carbonate is a pure form of limestone, the very substance gravestones are carved from. In stick form, calcium carbonate is better known as chalk used on blackboards. Since it is insoluable in water, calcium carbonate can only be assimilated by the body if there is a sufficient level of hydrochloric acid in the stomach. (Many Americans are deficient in HCL, especially the elderly.) If you insist on using it anyway, buy a pack of chalk instead; it is the same substance and cheaper than the pills! No calcium carbonate in chalk or any other form is recommended.

Good Sources of Calcium

> **Calcium Lactate** — good source if not allergic to milk

> **Calcium Gluconate** — good source

> **Calcium Orotate** — over priced but good source

> **Calcium Chelate** — good source

The author prefers the Orotate or Chelate forms for best assimilation. Recommendations for dosages are: PMS or post menpausal women—1000mg, otherwise 500mg per day is sufficient. Men can take up to 500mg per day.

Calcium supplements are best absorbed on an empty stomach and since **calcium loss is increased while sleeping, bedtime is an excellent opportunity for best absorption.** Calcium, in large doses, will eventually deplete magnesium levels, and **calcium is not readily taken in by the cell unless accompanied by magnesium.** The cell prefers to maintain a ratio of two parts magnesium to three or four parts calcium. Asking the cell to accept straight calcium without magnesium, altering its cell normal ratios, the cell will tend to reject the unescorted calcium. Straight calcium supplements without magnesium, advocated by many doctors, the body will either deplete magnesium reserves from other organs in order to absorb the additional calcium or reject the calcium totally. **Magnesium Chelate or Orotate should be** taken in the morning with breakfast at a ratio of half of the amount of calcium taken at bedtime.

Vitamin D is important in the assimilation of calcium from the intestinal tract (see Vitamin D recommendation).

Note

The dosages recommended are based on the amount of **elemental** calcium (the part the body uses) contained in the supplement and not the total amount of calcium in the product.

Warning

Between the ages of twenty and fifty Americans lose up to **a third** (33⅓%) of the total calcium in their skeleton **without** being aware of it. Calcium deficiency is hard to detect. **Even in extreme depletions, the calcium level in the blood may remain normal since the bones can be robbed to supply the blood.**

COPPER

Copper is a trace mineral found in all body tissues. **Copper is essential for the absorption of iron** (very important to women) and its conversion into hemoglobin. **Without sufficient copper reserves, anemia is possible.**

Copper is also essential for the utilization of Vitamin C (see Vitamin C), which is vitally important to all the endocrine glands and the production of sexual hormones. Lack of copper can create fatigue and water retention.

Copper is also involved in amino acid (protein) metabolism which manufactures hormones. It is necessary for the production of RNA, needed by every cell fro glandular maintenance.

Cigarettes, birth-control pills, and copper I.U.D.'s elevate copper levels excessively, blocking the utilization of iron, zinc, and Vitamin C.

Symptoms of Copper Deficiency

Anemia
Fatigue
Edema (water retention)

Food Sources of Copper

Whole grains
Almonds
Pumpkin seeds
Green leafy vegetables
Liver
Prunes
Dried beans
Legumes
Sunflower seeds

Supplementation

Unnecessary. Although copper is an essential element of your glands, in excess, copper can be toxic as well as reducing utilization of iron, zinc, and Vitamin C. Eat a few handfuls of sunflower or pumpkin seeds to increase copper intake.

IODINE

Iodine is a trace mineral that aids in the development and functioning of the thyroid gland. Thyroxine is important in regulating the production of energy, promotes growth of the other glands, and stimulates the proper rate of metabolism of cells. **Beta-carotene is converted into Vitamin A and cholesterol is produced, due in part, to thyroxine levels.** Iodine is especially needed during pregnancy to stimulate fetal growth and development. Iodine is vital to brain function, including the pituitary, hypothalamus, and pineal glands. When iodine reserves are exhausted, cells in the brain are destroyed. **Either excess or defiency can damage the lining of the uterus.**

Symptoms of Iodine Deficiency

Weight gain
Slow mental reaction
Lack of energy
Goiter development
Hair loss
Sterility
Susceptibility to infections
Poor sense of smell
Stinging in the temples
Stiffness in the neck muscles
Hypothyroidism

Food Sources of Iodine

Sea vegetables — kelp, dulse, nori
Fish
Citrus foods
Pineapples
Watercress
Artichokes

Supplementation

Kelp or dulse tables (2-6 per day), with meals

IRON

Iron is essential to the human body and is present in every living cell. Iron exists in the body combined with protein to make hemoglobin (red blood corpuscles). Hemoglobin carries oxygen from the lungs to every cell in your body. Iron and oxygen are like the hand and the glove; one cannot be considered without the other. **Iron, itself, gives no energy, but because iron helps carry oxygen, the increased oxygenation of the cells creates vitality and energy.**

When blood is lost, iron is also lost and must be replaced by adequate dietary intake. **Women require more iron than men since menstruation causes significant loss of iron each**

month. Newborn infants require four times the amount of iron needed by adults, therefore pregnant and lactating mothers should take extra iron in their diets.

A reducing diet can result in a loss of iron. Iron and calcium are the two major dietary deficiencies of American women.

Because iron and oxygen are inseparable, without sufficient iron present in the body, oxygen cannot be utilized properly. An iron deficiency will cause anemia and **anemic persons are too tired to make love.** Plenty of iron in the blood **ensures** energy, virtility, a strong (iron) will, a keen mind, and an optimistic outlook.

Without sufficient iron our cells would suffocate and die. Oxygen is drawn to the body like a magnet when sufficient iron is available in the blood. Iron improves circulation, digestion, elimination. All the glands are supplied with nutrients and oxygen thanks to iron reserves. Adequate Vitamin C is required to absorb iron. **For sexual vitality, iron is a must!**

Symptoms of Iron Deficiency

> Iron-deficiency anemia
> Lowered resistance to infections
> Fatigue (rundown feeling)
> Headaches
> Constipation
> Brittle nails
> Poor memory
> Shortness of breath
> Poor complexion (no color in cheeks)
> **Lack of sex drive (no interest)**

Food Sources of Iron

> Apricots
> Almonds
> Beans
> Prunes
> All red, blue, and black berries

Cherries
Kelp
Dulse
Dried Fruits

Supplementation

Since iron tablets can cause constipation, there are few acceptable supplements available. Floradix, a natural iron, is the best. Amino acid chelates of iron are well absorbed.

Caution—inorganic iron, ferrous sulfate, will interfere with Vitamin E utilization. Organic forms of iron will not interfere.

MAGNESIUM

Approximately seventy percent of the magnesium in the human body is found in the bones along with the calcium and phosphorus. Magnesium promotes the utilization of other minerals, including calcium, phosphorus, sodium, and potassium. **Magnesium is a "relaxing" element.** It induces sleep, relaxes nerves, neutralizes dangerous toxins and impurities. Magnesium is vital to muscle contractions and relaxation, and therefore **is vital to the function of a healthy heart muscle.** Bones, glands of the brain, uterine lining, nerves, and ovarian membranes need magnesium. Without sufficient magnesium, life may seem uninteresting and unimportant. **There can be an indifference to sexual activity with a general laziness regarding activity of any kind.** Depression, irritability, muscle tremors, or twitching, and menstrual imbalances are involved when this vital mineral is deficient.

Magnesium is vital to the contraction of the glands in order to release sex hormones. Frigidity, lack of interest in sex, and fear of sexual activity may accompany magnesium deficiency. Vitamin B_6 is essential to the proper absorption of magnesium in the body. Magnesium is stripped from many of our foods through processing. Chronic alcoholism depletes this precious mineral also. Calciforol, synthetic Vitamin D_3, tends to bind magnesium and carry it out of the body. Therefore, pasteurized milk and cheese tend to contribute to a deficiency of magnesium.

Symptoms of Magnesium Deficiency

Apprehensiveness
Hypertensitivity
Nervous system exhaustion
Muscle twitching
Confusion
Disorientation
Depression
Indigestion
Calcium deficiency

Food Sources of Magnesium

Figs
Lemons
Oranges
Grapefruit
Almonds—other nuts
Yellow corn
Apples
Dark green vegetables
Whole grains

Supplementation

Magnesium Chelate (good source)

Magnesium Orotate (good source) — Taken at a ratio of 1 milligram of magnesium for every 2 milligrams of calcium. For instance: 1000mg of calcium, 500mg of magnesium.

Caution—Magnesium **should not** be taken after meals since it neutralizes stomach acids. For best absorption, take half as much magnesium as calcium. **Take magnesium in the morning on an empty stomach and calcium at bedtime on an empty stomach.**

POTASSIUM

Potassium constitutes .0225% of the total mineral content of the body and is found primarily in the intracellular fluid. Potassium is **critical to maintain heartbeat.**

Roles of Potassium

1. Muscle contraction
2. Maintains proper alkalinity of the body fluids
3. Carries off fluids in lymphatic gland congestion
4. Regulates water balance
5. Assists in conversion of glucose to glycogen (sugar stored in liver)
6. Stimulates kidneys to eliminate body wastes
7. With phosphorous sends oxygen to the brain
8. With calcium regulates neuromuscular activity
9. Maintain heartbeat

Potassium deficiency affects the brain cells early, and a person may not be aware of the deficiency until damage has already been done.

Causes of Deficiency of Potassium

Deficiencies of potassium are caused by excessive intake of sodium chloride (table salt), lack of adequate fruits and vegetables in the diet, profuse sweating for many days without adequate replacement, prolonged diarrhea and consumption of refined sugar, which causes large amounts of potassium to be used up in glucose metabolism. Hypoglycemia (low blood sugar) can cause potassium loss as can prolonged fasts, high protein or starvation diets, mental and physical stress, and carbonated beverages. If potassium deficiency continues, muscles will not receive the energy needed, and paralysis could result. **Potassium is considered very important for the prevention of female disorders since it stimulates the functioning of all endocrine glands.**

The **"house-wife syndrome,"** characterized by chronic

fatigue, insomnia, and tiredness in relation to housework and love making is heired by supplements of magnesium and potassium. Lack of potassium can cause high blood pressure, muscle weakness, and irregular sleep patterns.

Symptoms of Potassium Deficiency

>General weakness
>Impairment of nerves
>Muscle damage
>Poor reflexes
>**Sagging muscles**
>Memory loss
>Dizziness
>Confusion
>Constipation
>Slow and irregular heartbeat
>Carbohydrate intolerance
>**Swelling**
>**Water Retention**

Food Sources of Potassium

Nuts and Seeds — almonds, anise seeds, walnuts, sunflower seeds, sesame seeds, pecans

Grains and Beans — lentils, pinto beans, brown rice, lima beans

Vegetables — potatoes, Jerusalem artichokes, carrots, parsley, watercress, broccoli, tomatoes, leaf lettuce, celery, spinach

Fruits — bananas, dates, currants, grapes, oranges, peaches, apples, watermelon, apricots, blueberries

Fish — all scaled fish

Supplementation

A potassium complex of 99mg is the common supplement in health food stores and supermarkets.

A potassium supplement may be necessary for three to six months (100-200mg daily) if a high salt and/or sugar intake has been maintained for several years. After several months on potassium, a diet high in grains, fruits and vegetables coupled with an elimination of salt should be adequate to maintain potassium levels. **Potassium is a natural diuretic (eliminates water through the kidneys).**

SELENIUM

Selenium is a mineral found in minute amounts in your body. It has some important beneficial effects. **It protects against the toxic affect of cadmium and mercury (found in canned tuna fish).**

Selenium increases the effectiveness of the "fertility vitamin," Vitamin E. These two together are stronger than each separately. Vitamin E and selenium are usually found **together** in grains, nuts, seeds, and vegetables **provided** selenium is found in the soil where these foods are grown. **Selenium assures normal body growth and fertility.**

Males have a great need for selenium since half of the supply of selenium in the body concentrates in the testicles, seminal ducts of the prostrate gland, and is richly found in semen itself. Selenium and Vitamin E are very important in pregnancy. One quarter of infant deaths in the United States are associated with selenium and/or Vitamin E deficiency. Sufficient foods containing selenium and Vitamin E eaten during pregnancy would insure healthy milk during lactation. **Human milk has six times the amount of selenium and twice as much Vitamin E as cow's milk.**

Selenium is a natural antioxidant and helps preserve the elasticity of the skin and other tissues. It may also prevent certain types of cancers. **Selenium may increase resistance to disease by increasing the number of antibodies which fight infections. (The sex glands are included.)** Selenium has helped to prevent chromosome breakage in tissue cultures and damaged chromosomes can cause birth defects. Selenium helps slow down the aging process because it aids in stopping the oxidation and hardening of tissues. **Selenium also relieves symptoms of menopause such as hot flashes.**

Symptoms of Selenium Deficiency

> **Prostrate troubles**
> **Impotency**
> **Sterility**
> **Hormonal imbalances**
> **Pre-mature aging**
> **Loss of stamina**
> Flabby skin
> Wrinkles
> Vitamin E deficiencies
> Dandruff

Food Sources of Selenium

> Whole grains
> Raw nuts and seeds
> Fish
> Onion
> Garlic
> Broccoli

Supplementation

Available in microgram dosages of 25 to 100mcg. **Caution**: Toxicity is possible even with small dosages. Take 25 to 50mcg daily or as directed by a health practitioner.

ZINC

Zinc is an essential trace mineral. Zinc is a component in over 25 enzymes involved in digestion and metabolism. Since zinc is part of the enzyme needed to break down alcohol, most alcoholics are deficient in this important mineral. Zinc aids in the formation of insulin and so many alcoholics are also diabetics. **Zinc governs the ability of the muscles to contract.**

Zinc is very important for general growth and in proper development of the reproductive organs (testes and ovaries) and the normal function of the prostrate gland. The greatest amounts of zinc are found in the thyroid, pancreas, liver, retina of the eyes, and prostrate gland. **There is a very high concentration of zinc in the sperm and seminal fluid.** Zinc is needed in the synthesis of DNA (deoxyribonucleic acid) which is responsible for the genetic code for duplication of all cells (inherited traits).

Zinc in proper quantities insures the utilization of copper, iron, and Vitamin A. New studies indicate its importance in brain function (pituitary, hypothalamus, pineal) and in the treatment of schizophrenia. Without sufficient quantities of zinc, infections, wounds, and other injuries heal poorly.

Sterility and lack of maturity of the sex organs is attributed to a lack of zinc. The highest concentration of zinc in the entire body is contained in the prostrate gland.

Infertility can sometimes be prevented or corrected with additional zinc and other elements combined. Mother's milk, at the birth of the infant, has the highest amount of zinc as compared to latter stages of lactation. **Normal sexual function can be maintained in the life of a male or female if zinc levels, as well as other nutrient levels, can be maintained.** Most zinc is lost in food during refining and processing and commercially grown foods are generally produced in zinc poor soils. Oral contraceptives and alcohol reduce zinc levels in the body.

Symptoms of Zinc Deficiency

> **Excessive fatigue**
> **Infertility**
> **Sterility**
> **Prostate problems**
> **Impotency**
> Arteriosclerosis

Poor growth
Slow healing of wounds
Poor iron metabolism

Natural Food Sources of Zinc

Whole grains
Eggs
Almonds—and other nuts
Seeds of all kind
Ground mustard
Sunflower seeds
Pumpkin seeds—raw and saltless are especially rich
    in zinc
Unprocessed, organic foods will have important
    quantities of zinc.

VITAMINS

HOW VITAMIN A AFFECTS YOUR SEX LIFE

Vitamin A is fat soluble and requires fat as well as minerals to be absorbed. **Fat is necessary in the production of hormones.** Vitamin A aids in the growth and repair of the body tissues (including the glands), and helps maintain smooth, soft, skin (sex hormones are involved in maintaining youthful, wrinkle-free skin). Vitamin A improves skin conditions like acne, dermatitis, psoriasis and exema. Zinc, essential to sexual reproduction, is necessary to maintain normal blood levels of Vitamin A. Vitamin E, also essential to reproduction is needed for the adequate uptake of Vitamin A. Vitamin A prevents Vitamin C from oxidizing (destroyed) and Vitamin C is essential to the glands, especially to the hormones of the adrenals and pancreas. Vitamin A is necessary for the eyes to perceive light of various intensities and colors (aids the pineal). It helps balance the production of cortisone and other steroid hormones produced by the adrenals. It protects the mucous membranes of the mouth, nose, throat, lungs and genital areas thereby reducing the risk of infection. Vitamin A, recent studies indicate, facilitates the absorption of RNA (ribonucleic acid) in the liver and every nucleus of living cells (including the glands). RNA is a nucleic acid that transmits to each cell of the body instructions on how to perform so that life, health, and proper function can be maintained. **The thyroid helps regulate the conversion of carotene to Vitamin A.** Hypothyroidism (under active thyroid) or Hyperthyroidism (over active thyroid) are ailments that upset Vitamin A utilization.

Symptoms of Vitamin A Deficiency

Loss of taste and appetite
Night blindness
Susceptibility to infections
Dry and aged skin
Acne
Sties in eyes and frequent fatigue
Psoriasis and other skin problems

Food Sources of Vitamin A

Fish
Dairy
Carrots
Apricots
Green leafy vegetables
Broccoli
Mangos
Pineapple
Yellow squash
Peaches
Cherries
Sweet potatoes
Beets
Pure vegetable oils

Supplementation

Since people living in cities with high air-pollution are more susceptible to infections and colds than those in cleaner air, environments, Vitamin A becomes a **must vitamin**. Since it is a fat soluble vitamin it can be stored in the tissues of the body, making it potentially toxic. Taking fish oil Vitamin A supplementation forces the body to either utilize the vitamin or store the excess.

To lessen the potential danger of Vitamin A toxicity, **take the carotene form instead of fish oil**. The conversion of carotene into Vitamin A is only 50% at best. Unabsorbed carotene is excreted in the urine. Since the body has a choice with carotene and no choice with fish oil, the preferred and safest supplementation of Vitamin A is carotene. **Supplementing 10,000 I.U. to 30,000 I.U. of beta-carotene per day will permit your body to absorb up to 50% and excrete the rest.**

HOW VITAMIN B AFFECTS YOUR SEX LIFE

Because Vitamin B Complex is water soluable it is not stored in the body and must be replace daily. All B vitamins are co-enzymes that functions as catalysts to accelerate certain chemical reaction necessary to health. A co-enzyme can combine with an inactive protein to make an active enzyme. **Enzymes are necessary in the chemical reactions of the glands in the process of making hormones. Glands and hormones are formed by a combination of protein, fat, and carbohydrates from foods which are digested, absorbed, and assimilated with the help of thousands of these enzymes.** B vitamins are crucial to the function of the brain (hypothalamus, pituitary and pineal) and the central nervous system. (The nervous system effects the functioning of adrenals, thyroid, sex organs and hypothalamus).

The B vitamins include:
1. Vitamin B_1 (Thiamine)
2. Vitamin B_2 (Riboflavin)
3. Vitamin B_3 (Niacin)

4. Vitamin B$_5$ (Pantothenic acid)—important to the adrenal glands
5. Vitamin B$_6$ (Pyridoxine—important to all sex glands and hormone production, a natural diuretic
6. Vitamin B$_{12}$ (Cobalamin)

Recently discovered components of the B Complex family are biotin, PABA (para-aminobenzoic acid), folic acid, choline, and inositol.

Although specific B vitamins are needed by the glands to manufacture hormones and function properly, all **B vitamins have a synergistic (cooperative) effect in your body and therefore, are more potent together than when used separately.** Found abundantly in natural foods like grains, beans, nuts, seed, and vegetables, B Complex is in its full compliment of B-factors and in perfect balance. **Although it may be advisable to take individual B vitamins for specific glandular or hormonal imbalances, the isolated B-factors work only to the extent that they are combined with whole foods, complete with all the B vitamins.**

Symptoms of B-Complex Deficiency

Nausea
Exhaustion
Tenderness and weakness in muscles
Skin disorders
Cracks in corners of mouth
Swollen tongue
Loss of memory
Poor digestion
Diarrhea
Depression
Oily skin
Pernicious anemia
Brain damage
Paralysis

Besides B vitamin deficiencies caused by refined foods, a wide variety of drugs and medications also contribute to deficiencies. Aspirin, oral contraceptives, alcohol, narcotics and anticonvulsants are only a few of the numerous drugs that may lead to B vitamin depletion. The stress of modern living takes a great toll on the nerves, glands and hormones, all requiring B Complex supplementation. Stress increases the need for B vitamins.

Food Sources of B-Complex

Whole grains
Rice polishings
Fish
Beans
Almonds
Sunflower seeds—(raw and unsalted)
Pumpkin seeds—(raw and unsalted)
Sesame seeds—(raw and unsalted)
Green leafy vegetables
Egg yolks
Liver

Supplementation

Although high in B-vitamins, brewer's yeast is not recommended because of its allergy producing potential (yeast is a mold). A rice based B-complex supplement can be taken with meals; however, since the absorption rate of tablets is poor, even a large dose of 100 mg twice a day will only permit **some** to be absorbed.

The best B-complex supplement is the sublingual (under the tongue) administration which bypasses the diluting effects of the stomach, intestines and liver, giving results similar to B-complex injections. Only one company, **Sublingual Products International**, manufactures an allergy free **liquid** form for immediate absorption into the bloodstream. For information write: Better Health Publishers, 1230 Brown Trail, Bedford, Texas 76022, (817) 282-0277.

HOW VITAMIN C AFFECTS YOUR SEX LIFE

Vitamin C is water soluable, not stored, and must be taken on a daily basis. Vitamin C, or ascorbic acid, is known to relieve scurvy and was first isolated from lemon juice. Vitamin C is required for the production and maintenance of collagen, a protein that is the base of all connective tissue—skin, tendons, bones, and teeth. Collagen is the protein substance that heals wounds, mends fractures, and prevents bruises. **Together with sex hormones, Vitamin C keeps the skin tight, elastic, and wrinkle free. Cellulite is a condition compounded by poor sex hormone production and Vitamin C deficiency.** Vitamin C protects against infections of your glandular system. **Women lose much iron during menstruation and Vitamin C promotes the absorption of iron to help reverse the depletion.**

Vitamin C is directly involved in the release of the stress hormones—adrenalin and noradrenalin from the adrenal medula. **Under stress, Vitamin C is depleted, and if not replaced the adrenals will be unable to sustain the energy level of the body.** This vitamin is also important in the production of the thyroid hormones, thyroxin, which regulates body metabolism, weight, and temperature.

According to recent studies Vitamin C is protective, as are Vitamins A and E, against cancers of the breast, cervix, ovaries, testes, prostate, lungs, and colon. This important vitamin is essential to the biochemical functions of the brain and therefore is necessary in order to support the hypothalamus, pituitary, and pineal glands located in the brain. Without Vitamin C, muscles of the vagina, uterus, and testes, penis, and prostrate weaken. Vitamin C is essential in amino-acid metabolism **(compounds that build sexual hormones)** and the specific amino acids, important to the brain, phenylalanine and tyrosine (pituitary, hypothalamus and pineal).

Vitamin C, in conjunction with sex hormones, is helpful in retarding the aging process. Recent studies show Vitamin C to be necessary for cholesterol regulation. (Cholesterol is a steroid which is involved in sexual hormone production.)

Glands can be attacked by heavy metals, chemicals, drugs, insecticides, and other environmental pollutants which can hinder or even stop their function. **Vitamin C, in adequate quantities, can help detoxify these toxic substances.**

The overproduction of estrogen or oral administration of an estrogen drug will elevate copper levels and reduce Vitamin C concentration. **Adequate Vitamin C levels are necessary in order that normal ovulation takes place.**

Symptoms of Vitamin C Depletion

> Increased infection or colds
> Bleeding gums
> **Anemia**
> **Cellulite**
> Slow healing
> **Easy bruising and fatigue**
> **When taking oral contraceptives**

Food Sources of Vitamin C

Rose hips
Acerola cherries
Green peppers
Apples
Citrus
Potatoes
Berries
Green leafy vegetables
Tomatoes
Broccoli
Turnips
Brussel sprouts
Cauliflower

Supplementation

Most Americans systems are over-acidic and the taking of large doses of ascorbic acid form of Vitamin C may contribute to further acidification of the stomach and kidneys. Ascorbic acid in large amounts raises uric acid levels, and may cause gout symptoms and even kidney stones. **Most Vitamin C supplements sold in pharmacies, health food stores and grocery stores are ascorbic acid. The** label may read "Vitamin C with Bioflavinoids," but the Vitamin C is ascorbic acid! Within the human body, minerals like calcium, magnesium, sodium and potassium **buffer** acids. When a mineral combines with ascorbic acid, a complex called **ascorbate** is formed. The mineral has **effectively buffered** the free acid. Using a **calcium ascorbate supplement**, whereby the manufacturer has already combined the mineral calcium with Vitamin C, **has the benefits of calcium and the protective value of Vitamin C without the acid.** When taking Vitamin C in large doses (1,000mg - 3,000mg per day), the ascorbated form is the safest and best. The daily ingestion of Vitamin C is a wise protective measure.

HOW VITAMIN D AFFECTS YOUR SEX LIFE

Vitamin D is fat soluble, and therefore stored in the body, it is known as the "sunshine" vitamin. As sunlight strikes the skin, cholesterol and other oils (concentrated in the skin) can be made into Vitamin D as the sun and the oils interact on the surface of the skin. **Showering immediately after sunbathing washes away cholesterol and other oils necessary for Vitamin D synthesis.** Wait approximately a half hour before showering in order to allow the conversion to take place and Vitamin D to be absorbed from the skin into the blood stream. **Sunbathing between 7-10am and after 4pm are the best times.**

Vitamin D is important in the assimilation of calcium and phosphorus from the intestinal tract. These minerals are indispensible for **all** body functions and especially to the work of the parathyroid glands which regulate calcium levels in the blood, and the thyroid glands control metabolic rate. Vitamin D is essential to these sex glands. Severe deficiency of the vitamin creates rickets in children. Insufficient Vitamin D will contribute to osteoporosis due to its vital role in calcium metabolism. Insufficiency can contribute to the development of glandular cysts, vaginitis, premature aging, acne, and leg cramps.

Since Vitamin D or ergosterol is produced from cholesterol, as are the other major steroid hormones, some experts believe Vitamin D is a hormone, not a vitamin. Its structure is similar to the chemical structure of other steroid hormones. The steroid connection means that it is connected to hormone production, particularly in the pituitary, parathyroids, and adrenals. If Vitamin D is a steroid hormone, should it be added to foods? Vitamin D added to dairy products, beverages, baby foods, breakfast cereals, margarine, flour, and animal feeds results in a per-capita intake in the U.S. of 2,435 I.U. per day, or six times the recommended 400 I.U. per day. **I recommend that Vitamin D fortification of our food be stopped, since we can safely obtain all the Vitamin D we need by spending thirty minutes in the sunshine.**

Symptoms of Excess Vitamin D

Vitamin D is known to cause:

Heart attacks in animals
Raise blood cholesterol levels
Irritate blood vessel linings
Promote joint disease
Arthritis
Magnesium deficiencies
Mental retardation in newborn babies

Symptoms of Vitamin D Deficiency

Rickets

Food Sources of Vitamin D

Fish—halibut, herring and salmon
Sunflower seeds
Green leafy vegetables—natural Vitamin D

Avoid foods with synthetic Vitamin D_3 added, such as pasteurized milk and cheese.

Supplementation

One-half hour of sunlight is the best form. Take fish oil capsules of A and D 10,000 I.U. per day **only** when exposure to sunlight is restricted.

Deficiencies of Vitamin D cause rickets. Excess dietary intake of Vitamin D causes calcium to deposit in the soft tissues, resulting in calcification of the joints (arthritis), while exposure to the sunlight aids in the proper utilization of calcium, thereby reducing arthritic symptoms.

HOW VITAMIN E AFFECTS YOUR SEX LIFE

Vitamin E is fat soluble and stored in the body. It is a complex of compounds known as tocopherols, alpha-tocopherol, being the most active form. Vitamin E is well known to be antioxidant. An antioxidant prevents oxygen from converting unsaturated fatty acids, saturated fatty acids, and Vitamin A (important for the health of testicles and mucous linings of the uterus and vagina) into **peroxides** which could be cancer producing. By sparing oxygen from fats, Vitamin E helps supply the red blood cells with more oxygen which is carried to the heart, organs, and glands. Vitamin E, through its oxygen stimulating role, increases vitality and energy. **Vitamin E protects sex hormones from destruction by oxidation.**

Vitamin E is known as the **"reproductive vitamin," "anti-sterility vitamin"** and the **"sex vitamin"** because it is closely involved in many reproductive and sexual functions. Vitamin E is stored in the testes, uterus, adrenals, and pituitary glands as well as in the muscles. It increases male and female fertility. Deficiencies of this vitamin may cause degeneration of cells of the testicles. **The birth control pill may neutralize the effect of Vitamin E.**

Since male sterility is a growing problem in the U.S., it would be wise to increase foods rich in Vitamin E, as well as follow a program of supplementation. **Vitamin E relieves such symptoms of menopause as hot flashes and dizziness.**

Since this vitamin is effective in the healing and prevention

of scar tissue formation within the body, it may be helpful in healing the scaring associated with endometriosis. Vitamin E helps regulate the flow and frequency of menstruation.

Symptoms of Vitamin E Deficiency

> Inflammation of the pancreas
> **Wasting muscles**
> Abnormal fatty deposits in the muscles
> Faulty absorption of fat
> **Infertility**
> **Irregular menstruation**
> **Sterility**
> Anemia
> Edema
> **Hormonal imbalances**
> Kidney congestion
> Heart disease
> Cancer

Vitamin E deficiency also causes red blood cells to rupture and become more vulnerable to environmental pollutants and stresses.

Food Sources of Vitamin E

> Whole grains
> Nuts
> Seeds
> Vegetable oils

Supplementation

Vitamin E's ability to bring precious oxygen to the cells, to protect red blood cells from destruction by food and environmental poisons and to aid the body in protecting itself against cancer-causing rancid fats, are excellent reasons for making sure an adequate amount is received through diet and supplementation.

Of the seven forms of tocopherols, alpha-tocopherol is the

most active and powerful and has the greatest nutritional value.
Take 100 I.U. to 200 I.U. of alpha-tocopherols with a fat
containing meal for best absorption. Another form of
Vitamin E supplementation is one teaspoon of **fresh** wheat
germ oil or two capsules of the oil.

HOW VITAMIN F AFFECTS YOUR SEX LIFE

Essential fatty acids are also known as Vitamin F. **The
body cannot manufacture these essential fatty acids—linoleic,
linolenic, and arachedonic; therefore it must be obtained from
foods.**

Vitamin F is essential for respiration of the vital glands
and organs and facilitates oxygen in the bloodstream to all
endocrine glands. **It helps maintain resilience, flexibility, and
lubrication of all cells in the testes, ovaries, vagina, and penis.**
Vitamin F is essential for normal glandular activity,
especially of the adrenal glands and thyroid glands. This
vitamin cooperates with Vitamin D in making calcium
available to the tissues. It stimulates the conversion of beta-
carotene into Vitamin A. Fatty acids aid the functioning of
the reproductive system. Fatty acids are useful in preventing
prostate trouble. **If sufficient linoleic acid is taken, the other
two fatty acids can be synthesized.**

Symptoms of Vitamin F Deficiency

> **Dry vagina**
> Vitamin A deficiency
> **Ovarian problems**
> Weight gain
> **Fatigue**
> **Menstrual irregularities**
> Psoriasis
> Dermatitis
> Irritability
> **Prostratis**
> Obesity

Food Sources of Vitamin F

> Sunflower seeds
> Almonds
> Pecans
> Other seeds and nuts
> Avocados
> Vegetable oils

Supplementation

Capsules of 100 to 150mg strength made from linseed oil. Take with a fat containing meal for best absorption.

GENERAL DIRECTIONS FOR TAKING SUPPLEMENTS

1. Take supplements six days a week and rest on the seventh day.
2. Take supplements for three months, then discontinue for three months. One may create a dependency or even an immunity to supplements if taken too long. Resume supplements, if needed, after a three-month rest.
3. Take supplements with meals unless otherwise advised by your nutritionist.

IMPORTANT

Much of the public believes nutrition means taking vitamins. Because so many claims are made regarding vitamins' curative power, the United States has developed a multi-billion dollar vitamin industry. **Although vitamins and minerals are helpful and necessary for a healthy sex life, please remember that vitamins are not food.** I hear so many say, "I don't eat right, but at least I take supplements!" Be aware that a supplement does what the word implies, it

supplements a healthy diet. **Supplements do not and cannot replace a natural diet. It is not natural to take any pill.**

You cannot expect to be healthy living on coffee, donuts and supplements. Good health does not work that way. There are no magic bullets for wellness. If you eat a nutritious diet of grains, seeds, nuts, fruit, and vegetables and reduce your fat, meat, sugar and salt intake, the supplements you take will have a better absorption rate. A good diet improves digestion, absorption and assimilation of vital nutrients including supplements. **If you do not assimilate foods, you will not assimilate supplements.**

SUPPLEMENT YOUR SEX LIFE

Today, with the many brands, formulas, and multi's on the market, little attention is paid to the sexual differences between men and women in those formulas. Also little consideration is given to the over-fifty person whose nutritional support is very different form the under-fifty crowd. Following are formulas designed with the supplemental needs of these different groups as they relate to sexual nutritional needs.

MEN'S STAYING POWER PAK
(Under Fifty)

Vitamin B-Complex (rice based)—50mg per day
Potassium—99mg per day
Siberian Ginseng—1 capsule per day
Bee Pollen—1 capsule per day
Zinc Chelate—50mg per day
Selenium—25mg per day
Magnesium—100mg per day
Calcium Chelate—200mg per day
Vitamin E—200 I.U. per day
Vitamin A (beta-carotene)—10,000 units per day
Vitamin C (ascorbates)—1,000mg per day

WOMEN'S STAYING POWER PAK
(Under Fifty)

Vitamin B-Complex (rice based)—50mg per day
B_6—50mg per day
Folic Acid—5mg per day
Dong Quai—1 capsule per day
Evening Primrose—1 capsule per day
Potassium—20mg per day
Magnesium—250mg per day
Calcium Chelate—500mg per day
Vitamin E—200mg per dsay
Vitamin A (beta-carotene)—10,000 units per day
Iron (Floridix) or Chelate—1 capful a day or 30mg per
    day
Vitamin C—1,000mg per day

MEN'S GOLDEN PLUS PAK
(Over Fifty)

Potassium Complex—200mg per day
Hydrochloric Acid (HCL)—2 before protein meals
B-Complex (rice based)—50mg per day
Zinc Chelate—100mg per day
Lecithin—3 capsules per day
Vitamin F—1 capsule per day
Bee Pollen—2 capsules per day
Pumpkin Seed Oil—2 capsules per day
Siberian Ginseng—2 capsules per day
Vitamin A (beta-carotene)—20,000 units per day
Vitamin C (ascorbates)—2,000mg per day
Vitamin E—400 units per day
Chromium Chelate—50mcg per day
Calcium Chelate—500mg per day
Magnesium Chelate—250mg per day

WOMEN'S GOLDEN PLUS PAK
(Over Fifty)

Calcium Chelate—1,000mg per day
Magnesium Chelate—500mg per day
Potassium Complex—200mg per day
HCL—2 before protein meals
B-Complex (rice based)—50mg per day
B_6—100mg per day
Folic Acid—5mg per day
Licorice—1 capsule per day
Royal Jelly—1 capsule per day
Evening Primrose—2 capsules per day
Dong Quai—2 capsules per day
Iron Chelate or Floridex—1 capful per day or 30mg
        per day
Vitamin C (ascorbates)—2,000mg per day
Vitamin E—400 per day
Lecithin—3 capsules per day
Vitamin F—1 capsule per day

These supplemental recommendations are to be used with the OH! YES! Program of nutrition and exercise for best results. The suggestions are for those who are experiencing a lower sex drive or lack of interest. The vitamins, minerals and herbs are to be taken for a 90-day or three-month period.

3

Unsexy Foods: Full But Famished Syndrome

"With health everything is a source of pleasure; without it ... nothing else ... is enjoyable. It follows that the greatest of all follies is to sacrifice health for any other kind of happiness. ..."

—Schopenhauer

What's wrong with the "well balanced" diet that some continue to insist has all the nutrients our bodies need? The answer to this question lies in the poor quality of foods available to today's consumer.

Nutrient deficient soils, chemical and synthetic fertilizers, time required for shipping and storage, refining and processing, and finally treatment with chemical additives, deprive plants and animals of vital nutrients as they travel from the farmer to the consumer.

FACTORS INVOLVED IN THE DEVALUATION OF FOOD

Today's American soil is a far cry from the fertile earth the Indians relied upon for health and survival. Hundreds of years of continual planting, failure to rotate crops, failure to permit fields to lie fallow for a season, failure to add organic matter to build up soil and natural weathering agents have depleted the once rich earth of many essential minerals and trace elements.

The soil in thirty-two of the United States has a zinc content below the adequate level, which means that foods grown in that soil are low in zinc content. As I said in the previous chapter, zinc deficiency in animals and humans results in retarded growth, delayed sexual maturity, prostate disorders, loss of taste, Vitamin A malabsorption, and failure of wounds to heal properly. Other minerals and trace minerals such as chromium, selenium, and copper, not necessary to plant growth, and therefore not added to synthetic fertilizers create health problems in animals and humans eating foods grown on deficient mineral soils. The nitrates from the nitrogen in artificial fertilizers destroys Vitamin A, in plants, one of the essential vitamin needs of the sexual glands. (See chapter on minerals and vitamins.)

STORAGE

Foods already inferior from having been grown in a deficient soil continue to lose valuable vitamins and minerals while in storage. **For an example, even under the best of storage conditions, vegetables such as spinach, potatoes, lettuce, and fruits such as apples can lose up to fifty percent of their Vitamin C during warehouse storage.**

Because natural foods stored too long would not only lose important nutrients but would also spoil, decay or rot, another step in food handling has evolved.

PROCESSING AND ADDITIVES

Farmers and distributors sell their raw foods to processors who produce packaged products for the grocery stores. **Processing retards spoilage.**

Canned and frozen meats and vegetables, commercial breads and boxed cereals containing refined flour and sugar remain attractive and tasty on supermarket shelves for long periods of time. Pasteurization, a process which will supposedly destroy harmful bacteria, nevertheless extends the shelf life of milk products by weeks. In fact, pasteurized milk doesn't **sour**, it **rots** instead. The utilization of modern processing techniques said to be a **convenience** to the consumers is actually a devise for food manufacturers to extend the shelf life of otherwise "perishable" products. **The price paid for "convenience foods" amounts to an unhealthy depletion of the vital nutrients the body needs to maintain health, energy, sexual virility, and fertility.**

Have you ever wondered how frozen vegetables stay so green? During the freezing process, green vegetables may be scalded with the chelating agent EDTA, removing trace elements such as zinc, manganese, and calcium. Because these nutrients are removed, the vegetables **remain bright green** rather than turning **gray** when cooled. Because of the widespread use of EDTA in food processing, **Americans consume up to 100mg of this chemical per day, and the daily consumption of EDTA continues to remove zinc, manganese, and calcium, needed for hormone production from the body.**

Vitamin C in foods, invaluable for most sex glands and sex hormone needs, is easily oxidized by metal contamination during processing. The reason that a steel knife quickly becomes dull when slicing lemons is that iron from steel ends up in the lemon juice. Stainless steel is the least likely to oxidize Vitamin C.

Zinc and calcium are also removed during the processing of oils so the oils will appear lighter in color (oils are naturally dark due to these nutrients). **Other nutrients destroyed during normal oil processing are Vitamin E, Vitamin A, and lecithin, all important to sex glands, sex hormones, healthy menstrual cycle, fertility, pregnancy, and fatty acid metabolism. Vitamin E and lecithin, natural antioxidants (which help oil from going rancid), removed during processing, are replaced by synthetic antioxidants called "preservatives." The only refined vegetable oils on the market that are cold-pressed are sesame seed oil and virgin olive oil (Virgin** on the label means the **first** pressing of the olives).

While wheat contains an abundance of vitamins, minerals, enzymes, lipids and protein—all important to sexual vitality and

sex hormone production, in processing, wheat becomes a devitalized, tasteless food, nutritionally inferior to the whole wheat. When the wheat is milled into white flour, the bran and wheat germ, rich in nutrients (zinc, iron, and calcium and Vitamin E) for fertility and virility are extracted from the kernal. (See Chapter on "Sexy Foods: OH! YES! DIET.") Practically all the B vitamins, including B_6, which are needed for most sex gland functions and nerves are stripped away from the kernal along with the bran and germ. The removal of bran from whole wheat, strips the kernal of its fiber, indispensible for good elimination. Refined or processed carbohydrates containing little bran or roughage, vitamins, or minerals, are nothing more than worthless empty calories which contribute nothing to sexual vitality. White bread contains 87.5% less fiber than whole-wheat bread, thus contributing to chronic constipation, diverticular disease of the colon and even colon cancer.

WHEAT: NUMBER ONE ALLERGY FOOD

Wheat is very high in gluten, a protein substance, and has become the number one allergy producing food in the United States. Remember making paper mache glue as children? What did we make this glue out of? White flour (refined wheat) and water. The stickiness of the glue results from gluten. Wheat contains more gluten than any other grain. This sticky gluten created mucus that can clog the bronchial tubes and lungs. There is nothing sexy about a runny nose! Allergy sufferers make poor lovers since they're either taking drugs or busy trying to breathe. Those with severe wheat allergies know what I'm saying about gluten, and the rest of you can try an experiment. Eliminate wheat from your diet for the next three months, then begin eating it again. Notice any of the symptoms mentioned earlier, as well as what appear to be actual cold symptoms? Remember that you are your own experimental laboratory. You can spend as much or as little time as you wish working in that laboratory.

How many times have you known someone who just

couldn't lose weight though they ate very little? Many of my clients, especially women, drop those extra pounds as soon as they eliminate wheat from their diets.

You may wonder what you can use in place of wheat since it is eaten so much in our culture. I recommend rice flour because it is gluten-free, delicious and lower in calories. Local supermarkets and health food stores carry rice flour as well as oat, soy, buckwheat and rye flour.*

Eating fresh, unprocessed whole grains and ripe, organically grown fruits and vegetables will help insure a full compliment of all vitamins and minerals needed for sexual health and vitality. **The Optimum Health for Youth, Energy and Sex (OH! YES! diet)** should include approximately thirty percent of total calories for a day in fresh vegetables (four helpings a day) and ten percent in fresh fruits (two whole pieces a day). The most important percentage of total calories (50%) should come from the **potent** grains, beans, nuts and seeds.

UNHEALTHY AND UNSEXY DIETARY SUBSTANCES

REFINED SUGAR

Virtually all commercial brands of boxed cereal, canned vegetables and fruit contain refined sugar. Most boxed cereals are 50% sugar. Half a cup of canned fruit contains four teaspoons of added sugar. Although most Americans refrain from adding refined sugar to foods, sugar is added to most processed and packaged foods.

---

*Whole wheat and white flour create the same allergy response.
**See wheat-free cookbooks listed in back of book.

REFINED SWEETENERS IN FOODS AND BEVERAGES

	Serving Size	Table Sugar Equiv. (tsp)	Sugar Calories (% of total calories)
SWEETENERS			
Pancake Syrup			
Karo Pancake & Waffle Syrup	1 tbs.	3.8 tsp.	100%
Golden Griddle	1 tbs.	3.3	100
Honey	1 tsp.	1.4	100
Table Sugar	1 tsp.	1	100
Molasses, Light	1 tsp.	0.8	100
SODA POP			
Shasta Orange Soda	12 oz.	11.8 tsp.	100%
Mountain Dew	12 oz.	100	
On Tap Root Beer	12 oz.	10.3	100
Pepsi-Cola	12 oz.	10	100
Shasta Cola	12 oz.	9.8	100
Coca-Cola	12 oz.	9.3	100
Sprite	12 oz.	9	100
Canada Dry Tonic Water	12 oz.	8.4	97.7
Canada Dry Ginger Ale	12 oz.	8	94.8
Shasta Ginger Ale	12 oz.	8	100
OTHER BEVERAGES			
Shasta Iced Tea	12 oz.	8.3tsp	100%
Hawaiian Punch	8oz.	6.5	100
Kool-Aid, you add sugar	8oz.	6.3	100
Kool-Aid, sugar added	8oz.	5.5-6	100
Nestle Hot Cocoa Mix	1oz.	5.8	84
HI-C, Grape	6oz.	5.5	88
Cranberry Juice Cocktail	6oz.	4.8	73
Nestea Iced Tea Mix, Sugar & Lemon	6oz.	4.3	97.1
Ovaltine Malt Flavor	4-5tsp.	4.3	77
Tang	4oz.	3.8	100
Gatorade	8oz.	3.5	100
Nestea Light	6oz.	2.8	100
CANDY			
Jelly Beans	10 pcs.	6.6tsp.	100%
Marshmallows	0.9oz.	4.8	100
M&M's			
Plain	1.7oz.	6.8	46
Peanut	1.7oz.	5.5	37
Candy Bars**			
Milky Way	2.1oz.	9	21
Snickers	2.0oz.	7.3	42
Mars Bar	1.7oz.	6.3	28
Royals	1.5oz.	6.3	47
$100,000 Bar	1.5oz.	5.3	42
Reese's Peanut Butter Cup	1.6oz.	5.3	31

**Roughly 10% of the sugar in chocolate bars is milk sugar (lactose).

	Serving Size	Table Sugar Equiv. (tsp)	Sugar Calories (% of total calories)
Nestle's Choco-Lite	1oz.	4	43
Nestle's Milk Chocolate	1oz.	4	43
Hershey's Milk Chocolate	1oz.	3.8	38
Candy Bars			
Hershey's Milk Chocolate, Almonds	1oz.	3.5	35
Krackel	1oz.	3.5	37
Nestle's Crunch	1oz.	3.5	37
Nestle's Milk Chocolate, Almonds	1oz.	3.5	37
Twix Caramel	0.9oz.	3.3	40
Mr. Goodbar	1oz.	3	31
Twix Peanut Butter	0.9oz.	2.5	31
Summit Cookie Bars	0.7oz.	2	28
Hard Candy			
Lifesavers	1pcs.	0.6	100
Gum			
Bubble Yum Bubble Gum	1pcs.	1.8	100
Hubba Bubba	1pcs.	1.5	100
Replay	1pcs.	1.1	98.9
Fruit Stripe	1pcs.	0.6	100
Wrigley, all stick varieties	1pcs.	0.6	92
Beech Nut	1pcs.	0.6	98

BAKED GOODS

	Serving Size	Table Sugar Equiv. (tsp)	Sugar Calories (% of total calories)
Keebler Cookies			
Old Fashioned Oatmeal	2pcs.	2.5	25
Pitter Patter	2pcs.	2.5	22
Rich 'n Chips	2pcs.	2.5	25
Vanilla Wafers	7pcs.	2.3	28
Coconut Chocolate Drop	2pcs.	2	19
Elfwich	2pcs.	2	29
Fudge Covered Graham Crackers	2pcs.	1.8	35
Kellogg's Pop Tarts			
Frosted Chocolate Vanilla	1 tart	4.8	35
Frosted Brown Sugar & Cinnamon	1 tart	3.5	27
Blueberry or Cherry Filled	1 tart	3.3	25
Twinkies	1 pkg.	8.4	47
Sara Lee Chocolate Cake	1.7oz.	4.2	37
Graham Crackers	2pcs.	0.9	25

DAIRY PRODUCTS

	Serving Size	Table Sugar Equiv. (tsp)	Sugar Calories (% of total calories)
Lowfat Yogurt, Fruit	1cup	7.5tsp.	52
Frozen Yogurt, whole milk	4oz.	6.1	62
Yogurt, flavored	1cup	4.1	34
Vanilla Ice Milk	½ cup	3.4	48
Dannon Frozen Yogurt, fruit	½ cup	3.3	50
Vanilla Ice Cream	½ cup	3.2	37
Dannon Frozen Yogurt, vanilla	½ cup	2.8	50
Chocolate Milk, 2% fat	1cup	2.7	24

	Serving Size	Table Sugar Equiv. (tsp)	Sugar Calories (% of total calories)
OTHER DESSERTS AND SWEET SNACKS			
Popsicle	1	4.5tsp.	100%
Orange Sherbet	½ cup	2.8	33
BREAKFAST CEREALS**			
General Mills			
Boo Berry	1oz.	3.3tsp.	47%
Count Chocula	1oz.	3.3	47
Franken Berry	1oz.	3.3	47
Chocolate Crazy Cow	1oz.	3	44
Pac-Man	1oz.	3	44
Trix	1oz.	3	44
Cocoa Puffs	1oz.	2.8	40
Lucky Charms	1oz.	2.8	40
Cheerios, Honey Nut	1oz.	2.5	40
Golden Grahams	1oz.	2.5	36
Buc Wheats	1oz.	2.3	33
Nature Valley Granola, Fruit & Nut	1oz.	2	25
Nature Valley Granola, Cinnamon & Raisin	1oz.	1.8	22
Nature Valley Granola, Coconut & Honey	1oz.	1.5	16
Nature Valley Granola, Toasted Oat	1oz.	1.5	18
Country Corn Flakes	1oz.	0.8	11
Total	1oz.	0.8	11
Total, Corn	1oz.	0.8	11
Wheaties	1oz.	0.8	11
Kix	1oz.	0.5	7
Cheerios	1oz.	0.3	4
Kellogg's			
Honey Smacks	1oz.	4	58
Apple Jacks	1oz.	3.5	51
Froot Loops	1oz.	3.3	47
Cocoa Krispies	1oz.	3	44
Sugar Corn Pops	1oz.	3	44
Frosted Flakes, Sugar	1oz.	2.8	36
Frosted Flakes, Banana	1oz.	2.5	36
Frosted Krispies	1oz.	2.5	36
Marshmallow Krispies	1oz.	2.5	29
Raisins, Rice & Rye	1oz.	2.5	29
Strawberry Krispies	1oz.	2.5	36
Corn Flakes, Honey & Nut	1oz.	2.3	33
Cracklin' Oat Bran	1oz.	2	27
Nutri-Grain, Wheat & Raisin	1oz.	2	23
Bran Buds	1oz.	1.8	40
Frosted Mini-Wheats, Sugar-Frosted	1oz.	1.8	25
Frosted Mini-Wheats, Apple-Flavored	1oz.	1.8	25
Most	1oz.	1.5	24
All-Bran	1oz.	1.3	29
40% Bran Flakes	1oz.	1.3	22

**Figures for cereals include naturally occurring sugar in raisins and other dried fruits.

	Serving Size	Table Sugar Equiv. (tsp)	Sugar Calories (% of total calories)
Kellogg's			
Crispix	1oz.	0.8	11
Product 19	1oz.	0.8	11
Rice Krispies	1oz.	0.8	11
Special K	1oz.	0.8	11
Corn Flakes	1oz.	0.5	7
Nutri-Grain, Corn	1oz.	0.5	7
Nutri-Grain, Wheat	1oz.	0.5	7
Post			
Super Sugar Crisp	1oz.	3.5	51
Honeycomb	1oz.	2.8	40
Raisin Bran	1oz.	2.3	40
Fruit 'n Fibre	1oz.	1.8	31
Raisin Grape Nuts	1oz.	1.5	24
40% Bran Flakes	1oz.	1.2	20
Grape Nut Flakes	1oz.	1.3	20
Grape Nuts	1oz.	0.8	12
Ralston Purina			
Cookie Crisp, Chocolate Chip Flavor	1oz.	3.3	47
Cookie Crisp, Vanilla Wafer	1oz.	3.3	47
Donkey Kong Junior	1oz.	3.3	47
Cookie Crisp, Oatmeal Flavor	1oz.	3	40
Sugar Frosted Flakes	1oz.	2.8	40
Raisin Bran	1oz.	2.3	36
Bran Chex	1oz.	1.3	18
Crispy Rice	1oz.	0.8	11
Corn Chex	1oz.	0.5	7
Corn Flakes	1oz.	0.5	7
Rice Chex	1oz.	0.5	7
Wheat Chex	1oz.	0.5	7
Quaker Oats			
Cap'n Crunch's Crunchberries	1oz.	3.3	43
Cap'n Crunch	1oz.	3	44
King Vitamin	1oz.	3	44
Quisp	1oz.	3	44
Cap'n Crunch's Peanut Butter	1oz.	2.5	31
100% Natural, Apples & Cinn.	1oz.	2	23
100% Natural, Raisins & Dates	1oz.	2.3	28
Life, Cinnamon	1oz.	1.5	22
100% Natural	1oz.	1.5	17
Life	1oz.	1.5	18
Shredded Wheat	1.3oz.	0.3	3
Puffed Rice	0.5oz.	0	0
Puffed Wheat	0.5oz.	0	0
MISCELLANEOUS			
Cranberry Sauce	1tbs.	1.5tsp.	96%
Skippy Peanut Butter	2tbs.	1.3	11
Ketchup	1tbs.	0.6	63

Sweetener amounts are manufacturers' approximations or are CSPI's estimates based on data supplied by manufacturers. Center for Science in Public Interest figures.

Although both natural and processed sugars do eventually break down into glucose, **the speed at which the sugar enters the bloodsteam is crucial.** Complex sugars, such as those in grains and fruits, digest slowly, causing no drastic elevation in blood sugar levels. However, concentrated or simple sugars enter the blood stream very quickly due to their elementary molecular structure (mono and disaccharides). **Simple sugars include white sugar, brown sugar, honey, molasses, maple syrup, and fructose in refined form.** Because simple sugars enter the bloodstream rapidly, quick energy lifts are experienced. However, if too much sugar reaches the blood too quickly, the amount of oxygen transported by the blood slows down, and the brain and extremities do not receive enough oxygen. **White sugar robs your cells of needed oxygen. You must have plenty of oxygen for sex.**

The pancreas helps maintain the proper blood sugar level through secretion of a hormone called **insulin**, which transports excess sugar to the liver where it is converted into glycogen. Glycogen is stored in the liver and muscles for release when your energy or blood sugar is low. With the aid of the adrenal glands, glycogen is then converted back into glucose. The adrenal glands secrete a hormone called epinephrine or adrenaline, which when combined with stored glycogen, produces glucose to raise blood sugar levels. Your body has the capacity to either lower blood sugar (insulin) or raise blood sugar (glycogen and adrenaline) as needed.

The average American eats 120 to 150 pounds of refined white sugar a year. Your pancreas was not designed to constantly secrete large amounts of insulin in order to reduce high levels of processed white sugar in your bloodstream. **If your pancreas is forced to over-produce insulin for an extended period of time (20-30 years), you run the risk of damaging the insulin producing mechanism.** Diabetes is a condition where too little insulin is produced and sugar levels in the blood remain too high. Amputation of arms and legs, as well as blindness due to circulatory problems (remember excess sugar blocks oxygen transportation) are some tragic results of diabetes.

Eight out of every ten cases of diabetes in the U.S. are Type II or the adult-onset type. **A diabetic (high sugar) condition is created by eating refined white sugar.** According to the book, *Sugar Blues*, the first step leading to diabetes (high blood sugar) is **low** blood sugar as a result of long-time insulin overproduction. **Your pancreas will exhaust itself after years of trying to counteract excess refined sugar intake,** eventually causing diabetes.

If you have symptoms such as depression, nervousness, irritability, loss of memory, sudden fatigue, dizziness, headaches, sweet craving, protein cravings, blurred vision or mental confusion, it could mean you have low blood sugar or hypoglycemia.

Most people experience an increase in energy after eating a candy bar or other sugar product, only to feel an energy crash approximately 20 minutes later. The secretion of a large amount of insulin by your pancreas in order to quickly lower the blood sugar causes the low energy response. Mood swings, depression and fatigue are common during this crash period. **Low energy means you will have a lowered sex drive.**

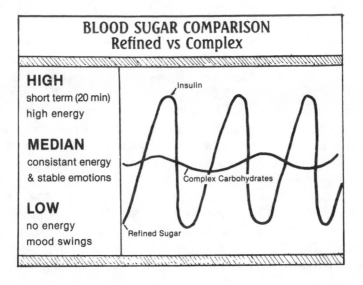

BLOOD SUGAR COMPARISON
Refined vs Complex

HIGH
short term (20 min)
high energy

MEDIAN
consistant energy
& stable emotions

LOW
no energy
mood swings

Insulin

Complex Carbohydrates

Refined Sugar

Besides finding refined sugar in pies, cakes, candies, and ice cream, we find it added to many other foods. Sugar constitutes more than one-third of the ingredients in commercial salad dressing, ketchups and boxed cereals. It is added to soups, gravies, hot dogs, and luncheon meats. **Sugar goes by many aliases: corn syrup or corn sweetener, fructose, dextrose, sucrose, raw sugar and brown sugar** (different name, same game). Some food labels list two or three different sweeteners in their ingredients. Even though these sugars do not appear as the number one or two ingredient, the sum of the sugars are greater than any other ingredient.

REFINED SUGAR IS A THIEF

All sugar eaten, whether natural or refined, requires B-complex vitamins, calcium and magnesium to aid in digestion. Natural carbohydrates, such as grains and fruit, contain enough of these nutrients to assist the body in their own digestion. Refining sugar (white or brown) removes these, and many other precious vitamins and minerals. **B-complex is taken from the nervous system and calcium and magnesium from the bones and teeth to digest refined sugars.** Consequently, refined sugar "**robs**" you of these needed nutrients resulting in "**raw**" nerves—nerve energy necessary for sex gland stimulation and endurance.

According to statistics, most of us can expect to have some form of osteoporosis or arthritis in our lifetime. Osteoporosis is the thinning of bones or removal of calcium from the bones. **One of the leading causes of osteoporosis is the use of refined sugar, which forces the body to use up its own calcium and magnesium storage.** As calcium and magnesium are removed from the bones, they end up in the soft tissues of the body, including the hair and the joints. This accumulation of calcium in the joints is commonly referred to as arthritis. Approximately 75% of men and women over 60 have some form of osteoporosis or arthritis. **Is it old age which causes these degenerative conditions, or the**

consumption of the thief called refined sugar?

Harmful effects of eating refined or simple sugars are the development of degenerative diseases such as diabetes, hypoglycemia, osteoporosis, and arthritis. **Complex carbohydrates, not refined sugar, are the time-released sugars the brain and cells need to function optimally.** As long as Americans do not eat complex carbohydrates in their diets, they will crave refined sugars. **The solution to breaking the sugar habit is to replace simple sugars with complex ones.** Start including grains like millet, buckwheat, brown rice, and oats in your diet every day, and your craving for candy bars, pop, and junk foods will decrease. **Saying "NO" to sugar is not sufficient to maintain good health: you must say "YES" to grains.** (See chapter on Sexy Foods: OH! YES! diet).

SALT

Even though salt is essential to your system, in excess it can be very dangerous. Adults need approximately 400mg or one-fifth of a teaspoon of salt daily to maintain optimum health and internal balance. The average American adult consumes two to two and one-half teaspoons of salt every day; more than ten times the bodily requirement. Salt excess in the American diet is derived from salt and/or sea salt. Both table salt and sea salt (99%-90%) contain sodium chloride. The over-consumption of sodium chloride depletes your body of needed potassium. Without enough potassium, symptoms such as loss of memory, mental confusion, heart palpitations and water retention may be experienced. **Women seem to be very sensitive to potassium loss and often experience swelling and weight gain.** Your kidneys are responsible for eliminating water and excess salt from your body. The kidneys filter all the sodium and potassium out of the bloodstream and with great precision, return the exact amount needed to the blood. Excessive amounts of salt overwork the kidneys, contributing to water retention and potassium loss. Such excess load on the kidneys will damage their delicate filtration system. **Dark circles and**

puffiness under the eyes are signs of overworked kidneys.

The connection between overconsumption of salt and hypertension is clear. More than 60 million Americans suffer from hypertension, and nearly one-half of the population over the age of 65 is affected by the condition. Too much salt can reduce the diameter of your arteries leading to high blood pressure. If you have ever seen meat cured by salt, you know that the salt pulls the water and blood out of the meat (shrinks meat). Excess salt in the bloodstream will pull the fluid out of an artery causing it to constrict or become smaller. In other words, as the diameter of the artery becomes smaller, the blood pressure increases.

High blood pressure, or hypertension, is the most significant factor influencing both strokes and heart attacks in the United States, Japan and other industrialized countries. The Japanese probably consume more salt than any other culture in the world. Their diet includes nearly three teaspoons of salt each day, consumed in foods such as fish, pickled vegetables and soy seasoned rice (1,029 mg. per tablespoon). Japan leads the world in hypertension, and it comes as no surprise that their leading cause of death is strokes. In the United States, approximately 550,000 strokes occur annually, resulting in an estimated 162,000 deaths while 1,250,000 heart attacks result in 550,000 deaths. In simpler cultures like Hunza, Abkhazia (Russia) and Vilcabambas (Equador), as well as the tribes of New Guinea, the Amazon Basin, the highlands of Malaysia, and rural Uganda, little or no salt is eaten and hypertension does not exist.

REMEMBER

1. One-half of all salt for Americans is added during processing.
2. **The more processed a food, the higher the salt content.**
3. Choose food labeled low sodium or salt-free.
4. Replace carbonated drinks high in sodium with unsweetened fruit and vegetable juices and bottled water.

5. Cheese is loaded with salt. Replace with low fat, plain yogurt.
6. Nuts should be raw and **unsalted.**
7. **Buy unsalted butter.**

PROTEIN

A baby triples its weight in the first year of life, growing from seven to 21 pounds! Since protein is necessary for growth, one would think a baby's incredible increase in size means there is a substantial percentage of protein in mother's milk. **Actually, nature provides only 3-6% protein in human milk!** During a period of your life when protein is in great demand, you're on a diet that provides 3-6%. We need far less protein than we think. According to the Recommended Daily Allowance for protein, the older we become, the less protein we require. By the time we reach 19 years old, our protein requirement is only .8 grams per 2.2 pounds. For instance, if I weighed 110 lbs., I would divide 110 by 2.2 which works out to 50. If I multiply .8 grams times 50, I have an answer of 40 grams. A 110-pound person needs 40 grams of protein per day unless pregnant or lactating. If you are pregnant, add 30 grams of protein; if you are lactating, add 50 grams of protein.

HOW MUCH IS ENOUGH?

The Recommended Daily Allowance (R.D.A.) for total protein for one day is computed by using the following equation:

$$2.2\,\overline{\smash{\big)}\,\text{your weight} \times .8\,\text{grams}} = \text{Protein required for one day}$$

In healthy cultures of the world, the average protein intake is 30-60 grams per adult per day. **The RDA for the average adult in the United States is 45 grams,** a figure very consistent with the quantity of protein eaten in healthy cultures. **Most Americans eat two to three times the quantity of**

protein required by the RDA (45 grams) to maintain protein balance. For instance, a Standard American Diet (S.A.D.) for breakfast is two eggs, a three-ounce slice of ham or bacon, a glass of milk, and two slices of toast, which contribute **47 grams** of protein. An average breakfast alone would provide adequate protein for an entire day.

The S.A.D. for lunch would be a quarter pound of hamburger with a slice of cheese, totaling **40 grams** of protein. This amount almost qualifies as enough for the entire day.

Since meat is a favorite protein of Americans, such a dish for dinner is a likely choice. Steak and potatoes (eight oz. steak and one medium potato) provide **58 grams** of protein. Computing the protein content of "three-quarters' a day in the above mentioned menu provides **145 grams** of protein. This hypothetical, but not unrealistic, menu constitutes three times as much protein as the RDA requirement!

PROTEIN SPARING DIETS

Sacrificing protein requirements in order to create energy or glucose results in protein depletion. **Using protein to provide glucose instead of carbohydrates is like using dollar bills to make a fire instead of newspaper.** Although protein deficiencies are almost unheard of in the United States, protein excesses are commonplace. The harmful effects of excess protein are well-documented.

RISKS OF OVER CONSUMPTION OF PROTEIN

1. Diets high in protein increase the body's loss of calcium (ratio of calcium to phosphorous in meat is 1:20 rather than the ideal 2:1). Excess phosphorous depletes calcium.

2. The higher a person's intake of meat and dairy, the more fruits, vegetables and grains will be crowded out of the diet, causing important nutrient deficiencies.

3. Because the human body has no adequate system for eliminating large quantities of excess protein, the liver and kidneys overwork to accommodate the overload (protein overload effect).

4. Excess protein accumulates on the walls of the tiny capillaries leading to cells reducing the capillaries' ability to give adequate nutrients to the individual cells (cell starvation).

5. Excess protein is accompanied by large amounts of fat associated with a high risk of atherosclerosis or hardening of the arteries.

Eat poultry and fish a few times a week and add whole grains, legumes and beans generously to your diet.
ARE YOU GETTING ENOUGH PROTEIN? THE DANGER IS IN TOO MUCH, NOT TOO LITTLE.

FATS

More than half of all food dollars are spent outside the home, primarily in fast food chains across America, over $10 billion dollars each year. The popularity of these fast food restaurants lies in their speed, uniformity and convenience **rather** than the food's nutritional value.

At lunch time, millions of Americans stand in lines at burger places so that in five minutes they are safely at a table, bench or car gulping down a burger, fries and a shake.

Even though there are no surprises at the cash register, three hidden surprises are known:

1. A burger, fries, and a shake provide half the calories needed for an entire day by a normal adult and with little nutritional value (empty calories, too).

2. These fast foods provide two or three times the amount of salt a normal person would need for a whole day.

77

3. Over half the calories are provided by fat, usually in a rancid form (fried or roasted).

Because of the empty calories and over abundance of fat contained in these fast foods, one in four Americans are overweight, and children are at least 20% heavier than their parents at the same age.

The Standard American Diet (S.A.D.) with almost half of its calories from fats is creating epidemics of obesity and pre-occupation with one's weight! The American Cancer Society and the National Cancer Institute warns people of the dangers of excess fat contributing to incidences of cancer. The Heart Association warns of the dangers of saturated fats leading to heart disease.

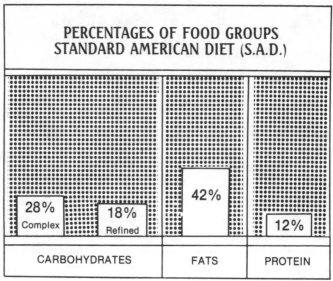

PERCENTAGES OF FOOD GROUPS
STANDARD AMERICAN DIET (S.A.D.)

CARBOHYDRATES		FATS	PROTEIN
28% Complex	18% Refined	42%	12%

Source: Dietary Goals for the U.S. Select Committee on Nutritional & Human Needs U.S. Senate.

Fats are called **lipids**, a general term for fats. There are three forms of fats called triglycerides, phospholipids (lecithin), and sterols (cholesterol), with triglycerides making up over 95% of all the fat in foods and in our bodies.

Fat in food includes oils, butter, margarine, and fat

visibly seen in meats. However, invisible fats are hidden in foods such as meats, nuts, cheese, pastries.

There are no documented toxic effects of essential unsaturated fatty acids (Vitamin F) but **excessive amounts of saturated fats can cause elevated cholesterol levels, plating, and hardening of the arteries, obesity, and cancer.**

Approximately twice as many unsaturated fatty acids as saturated fatty acids each day are needed for arterial health. The daily calories from fat in the diet should only be 20% to satisfy the requirements for fat.

Unfortunately we eat 40% to 50% fat in the Standard American Diet (S.A.D.) and most of those calories are saturated fats from meats, cheese and other animal sources. Most of the unwanted calories and saturated fat is eaten at these fast food restaurants. Following are the amounts of calories, fats and salt contained in some of these selected fast foods.

NUTRITIONAL CONTENTS OF
SELECTED FAST FOODS

	Calories	Fat (Pats*)	Fat (Percent of calories)	Sodium (mg)
MCDONALD'S				
Hamburger	255	2.6	35	520
Chicken McNuggets	314	5.0	54	525
Filet-O-Fish	432	6.6	52	781
Big Mac	563	8.7	53	1,010
Sausage Biscuit	582	10.4	61	1,380
ROY ROGERS				
Plain Potato	211	0	0	65
Potato w/Oleo	274	1.9	24	161
Roast Beef Sandwich	317	2.7	29	785
Crescent Roll	287	4.7	56	547
Potato w/Broccoli 'n Cheese	376	4.8	43	523
Crescent Sandwich w/Sausage	449	7.7	59	1,289
Crescent Sandwich w/Ham	442	7.5	58	1,192
WENDY'S				
Pasta Salad (½ cup)	134	1.6	40	400
Chicken Sandwich on Wheat Bun	320	2.6	28	500
Taco Salad	390	4.8	40	1,100
Broccoli & Cheese Potato	500	6.6	45	430
Cheese Stuffed Potato	590	9.0	52	450
HARDEE'S				
Chef's Salad	272	4.2	53	517
Chicken Filet Sandwich	510	6.9	46	360
Shrimp Salad	362	7.7	72	941
Bacon Cheeseburger	686	11.1	55	1,074

NUTRITIONAL CONTENTS OF
SELECTED FAST FOODS (Continued)

ARBY'S

Roasted Chicken Breast (no bun)	254	1.9	25	930
Broccoli & Cheese Potato	540	5.8	37	480
Mushroom & Cheese Potato	510	5.8	39	640
(Fried) Chicken Breast Sandwich	584	7.4	43	1,323
Sausage & Egg Croissant	530	9.3	59	745

LONG JOHN SILVER'S

Baked Fish w/Sauce	151	0.5	12	361
Mixed Vegetables	54	0.5	33	570
Corn on the Cob	176	1.1	20	0
Coleslaw	182	4.0	74	367
Fish w/Batter (2 piece)	404	6.4	53	1,346

BURGER KING

Veal Parmigiana	580	7.1	42	805
Bacon Double Cheeseburger	600	9.3	53	985
Specialty Chicken Sandwich	690	11.1	55	775

JACK IN THE BOX

Shrimp Salad (no dressing)	115	0.3	8	460
Taco Salad	377	6.3	57	1,436
Chicken Supreme Sandwich	601	9.5	54	1,582

KENTUCKY FRIED CHICKEN

Breast (Original Recipe)	199	3.1	53	558
Extra Crispy Dark Dinner**	765	14.2	63	1,480

*Pats-of-butter equivalent. A pat of butter contains 3.8 grams of fat.

**Includes drumstick, thigh, mashed potatoes, gravy, coleslaw, and roll.

REMEMBER

A gram of fat has twice as many calories as a gram of protein or a gram of carbohydrate.

> 1 gram of Protein = 4 calories
> 1 gram of Carbohydrate = 4 calories
> **1 gram of FAT = 9 calories**

Labels are very misleading when the fat content of processed foods is given. For instance if a label reads:

> Each serving of x ounces is 100 calories
> 4 grams of Protein
> 6 grams of Carbohydrates
> 7 grams of Fat

Although seven grams of fat seems low when compared to 100 calories, remember to multiply 7 times 9 calories. For every 100 calories of this food, there are 63 calories of fat!

If the intake of saturated fats is too high, as it is in the U.S., a deficiency of linoleic acid can develop **even if** other oils are included.

Restricting red meats, milk, eggs and cheese while increasing the use of vegetable oils like olive and sesame oil as well as other vegetable oil containing foods, will insure a healthy balance of low cholesterol, high essential fatty acid level in your body.

The need for unsaturated fatty acids is met when two tablespoons of vegetable oil are taken each day. However, eating raw almonds, corn, raw sesame seeds, raw pumpkin seeds and raw sunflower seeds will also provide the needed essential fatty acids.

POLYUNSATURATED FATS ARE NOT SAFE

Polyunsaturated oils such as sunflower and corn may actually cause cancer since polyunsaturated oils go rancid the easiest of all oils. Rancid oils are implicated in free radical production in the body. Free radicals interfere with normal cellular growth and can cause cancer growth in cells. **Mono-unsaturated** olive oil and certain fish apparently do not (discussed in another chapter).

"Animal studies," according to Dr. Henry Blackburn, director of Laboratory of Physiological Hygiene at the University of Minnesota, demonstrates that diets high in polyunsaturated fats, such as corn and safflower oil, lead to more tumors than diets high in other fats.

The EPA and DHA oils, known as omega-3, fatty acids are the beneficial fats found in salmon, mackeral, and herring which help reduce the rate of heart disease and cancer. Keeping fat levels below 20% of total calories and primarily 40-50% from monounsaturated and omega-3 oils rather than saturated or even polyunsaturated oils is a healthy practice.

High fat diets will definitely interfere with your sex life. If arteries are clogged with fat, less blood and nutrients will be delivered to areas of the body needed for adequate sexual activity. Lower your total fat intake to raise your libido!

Fatty Acid Composition of Oils and Fats

% of Total Fatty Acids

Saturated	Monounsaturated	Polyunsaturated

Safflower Oil
| 9 | 13 | 78 |

Sunflower Oil
| 11 | 20 | 69 |

Corn Oil
| 13 | 25 | 62 |

Olive Oil
| 14 | 77 | 9 |

Soybean Oil
| 15 | 24 | 61 |

Peanut Oil
| 18 | 48 | 34 |

Sockeye Salmon Oil
| 20 | 55 | 25 |

Cottonseed Oil
| 27 | 19 | 54 |

Lard
| 41 | 47 | 12 |

Palm Oil
| 51 | 39 | 10 |

Beef Tallow
| 52 | 44 | 4 |

Butterfat
| 66 | 30 | 4 |

Palm Kernel Oil
| 86 | 12 | 2 |

Coconut Oil
| 92 | 6 | 2 |

Sources: *Handbook No. 8-4* and Human Nutrition Information Service, U.S.D.A.

WARNING

If you think that you are eating a low saturated fat meal by selecting chicken nuggets and fish sandwiches, think again. The fish and chicken are generally cooked in **beef tallow**, the fat trimmed from meat and made into shortening. Tallow is high in saturated fatty acids and can elevate the cholesterol levels in the blood.

Dr. Sacks, at Harvard Medical School, found McDonalds, Burger King, Wendy's, Arby's, Hardee's and Popeyes were frying their French fries in beef tallow. The fatty acid profiles, according to *Science Digest*, of Chicken McNuggets and Filet-O-Fish were more like beef than of chicken or fish. In 1984, 1.4 billion pounds of edible beef tallow was consumed in the U.S., mostly for frying.

Remember, the Natural Cancer Institute recommends lowering total fat intake because countries with traditionally low-fat diets seem at lower risk for cancer of the breast, prostate, and pancreas (all endocrine glands). This is easily accomplished by limiting red meats and dairy products in your diet and substituting fish, chicken, turkey, grains, beans, nuts, and seeds.

SYNTHETIC HORMONES IN MEAT

Modern technology has developed a way to raise a calf (90 pounds at birth) into a full grown cow (2,000 pounds at maturity) in only six months instead of the normal maturing time of eighteen months. This miraculous (or monstrous) accomplishment is achieved by administering **growth hormones,** such as diethylstilbesterol (DES) and other synthetic steroid hormones. These synthetic hormones are primarily forms of estrogen, which stimulate the endocrine glands, particularly the pituitary, to develop or mature and fatten the cattle in one-third of the natural growing period for cattle. If these same estrogen hormones that are given to cattle were injected into six-year-old girls, they would develop symptoms of precocious puberty, premature sexual development. A young girl would grow pubic hair, begin to menstruate, develop breasts, and commence bone development that precludes normal growth.

Although synthetic estrogen hormones such as DES and other steroids used by food manufacturers and farmers have been investigated by the Food and Drug Administration and the U.S. Department of Agriculture, no conclusive evidence of their danger has been found. I must observe, however, that elementary and junior high school girls today appear to be much more developed at years eight through twelve than when I attended school some twenty-five years ago. Some experts suggest that hormone traces found in meat, chicken, turkey, eggs, milk, and cheese are responsible.

How can female hormones in meat effect men? Synthetic estrogen, even in tiny amounts, can cause men to develop female characteristics. Could the eating of meat containing female hormones be a contributing factor to the increase of male homosexuality?

Steroids in meat may be contributory of increasing numbers of men and women developing problems of infertility and hormonal imbalances.

As if the hormones weren't enough of a problem, when animals mature at an artificially accelerated growth rate, the immune system does not develop properly. Consequently, cattle and poultry producers frequently administer antibiotics such as penicillin and tetracycline to "improve" the animals' low resistance to infection. The concern is not only that by injesting antibiotics in meat on a daily basis we may destroy the body's ability to produce antibodies (healthy bacteria) to fight infection, but also the possibility that antibiotics fed to animals can result in "drug resistant bacteria" appearing in the meat. These drug resistant bacteria such as almonella, can cause infections in the people who eat the meat. Because 18 million pounds of antibotic feed are consumed by animals every year in the United States, the development of antibiotic resistant bacteria is a matter of serious concern. Since the early 1950s low dosages of hormones and antibiotics have been routinely added to the feed of cows, chickens, turkeys and pigs. **If you eat enough milk, poultry, and meat, you can be certain you receive a hefty dose of these steroids and antibiotics!** Another 17 million pounds of the same antibiotics are given to Americans by their doctors. **The abuse of antibiotics over the last thirty years is resulting in an alarming and ever-increasing number of bacteria that are resistant to antibiotic drugs.** Perhaps the increased frequency of diseases related to a faulty or depleted immune system: cancer, AIDS, herpes, colds, and influenza are at least partially the result of eating meat containing these antibiotics.

Synthetic female hormones in meat, poultry, and milk could interfere with the levels of the hormone, testosterone, which is the stimulus of sexual libido in both men and women. **A man who looks upon a thick steak as a source of strength and virility may actually be contributing to his own wilting potency.** In 1929, studies indicated that American men average 100 million sperm per cubic centimeter of semen. Recent studies show a drop to 60 million sperm per cubic centimeter. Dr. Ralph Dougherty, professor of chemistry at the University of Florida, studied the fertility of 1,000 male students and found 23 percent were below 20 million sperm per cubic centimeter, subnormal fertility. I, along with other concerned individuals and groups would like to see a nationally funded study to measure the sperm counts of

American men. Since women can have regular pap smears, breast checkups, and mammograms, certainly men could be routinely examined for sperm count. This study and follow-up sperm tests would give a clear and precise diagnosis that would form a basis from which to encourage the Food and Drug Administration and the U.S. Department of Agriculture to stop adding synthetic hormones to our foods.

Alternative—Fish, discussed in the chapter **Sexy Foods**: AH! YES! Diet, is a good source of protein, cholesterol lowering EPA oils, and virtually free of the hormones and antibiotics routinely fed to cattle, hogs and poultry. If you are a confirmed meat eater, despite the hard-to-digest protein and high fat content, at least find meat that is not fed synthetic female hormones and antibiotics.

4

Drugs: A Downhill Road

"Before you can break out of prison, you must first realize you are locked up."

—Dr. Robert Anthony

THE EFFECTS OF DRUGS ON YOUR SEXUAL HEALTH

Both legal and illegal drugs threaten the health of the liver, pancreas, and sexual organs. Impotence, infertility, and exhaustion are the aftermath of habitual use. They are not recommended for those interested in optimum health and sexual activity.

In the last three generations, medicine has made a hundred and eighty degree turn away from successful centuries-old traditions of natural therapies such as nutrition, herbs, and common sense in favor of an expensive array of invasive synthetic chemical drugs. These drugs constitute a major threat to public health.

It is the **"legal"** drugs which are prescribed or sold over the counter that especially concerns me, because of their nearly universal use. **Americans are programmed to trust in and consume drugs without question** of their potential hazards.

The legal drug industry grosses $20 billion in sales and over $2 billion in annual profits. **Expenditures for drugs comprise twelve percent of the total health care costs.** In a report prepared by the Food and Drug Administration and the independent National Academy of Sciences, seven out of the ten most commonly prescribed drugs "either lack evidence for efficiency or are the second or third choices for their purpose. Of the remaining three, it is impossible to avoid the conclusion that they are overprescribed." **Darvon,** a pain killer, is the country's **number-one cause of overdose death,** more frequent than heroin or barbituates overdoses.

In addition to the ineffectiveness of many prescription drugs, many can cause addiction, illnesses, and even premature deaths. Eight thousand people die in hospitals from medically prescribed drugs. **One-seventh** of all hospital stays are devoted to the care of drug toxicity.

Uppers (Antidepressant)	Downers (Tranquilizers)
Elavil	Valium, Lithium
Triavil	Phenobarbital
Sinequan	Meprobamate
	Dolmane

These commonly prescribed drugs are either antidepressants or tranquilizers. They supposedly relieve one or more of the symptoms of depression, anxiety, tension, fatigue, agitation, or insomnia. Most of these drugs affect the brain and central nervous system. They alter the function of the pituitary, hypothalamus, thyroid, and adrenal glands, all vital to sexual activity. **Since their side effects can include diminished sex drive, lethargy, low or high blood pressure, drowsiness, dizziness, fluid retention. irregular menstrual cycles, nervousness, liver dysfunction, anemia, blurred vision, reduced sexual performance, hair loss, and general weakness, they are not recommended for anyone wanting to improve sexual activity and performance.**

Impaired absorption is a common mechanism by which drugs interfere with vitamin homeostasis. Certain drugs compete with vitamin needs. Different drugs deplete different vitamins, but the most common drug induced deficiencies include B_3 (niacin), B_6 (pyridoxine), Vitamin C, Vitamins A and D, and folic acid. All of these nutrients are important in sex gland function and performance. There is a growing concern regarding drug-induced malnutrition.

Prescription, over-the-counter, and recreational drugs all have one factor in common. **They all have harmful side effects. Even aspirin can kill.** The author suggests that every home have a **Physician's Desk Reference** (PDR), which will describe the benefits as well as the potential hazards of a drug your doctor prescribes for you.

Drugs, whether illegal, prescription, or over-the-counter, weaken glands, deaden nerves, create vitamin-mineral deficiency and have a detrimental effect on your sex life. **In fact, studies indicate that drugs can deplete your sexual energy, impairing sexual performance and lessening your sexual pleasure and enjoyment.**

MARIJUANA

Many people in the U.S., particularly young people, are using marijuana as an alternative to alcohol. The number of people using marijuana grew from half a million in 1971 to over three million in 1980. This drug alters the sensations of hearing, touch, taste and smell. It produces a heightened desire for food, especially sweets (the munchies). Although research on marijuana indicates that apparently it doesn't change the blood glucose level, it definitely increases the demand for junk foods such as ice cream, cookies, chocolate, pies, cakes, and candy. Because it encourages the increased consumption of refined sugar, regular use of marijuana will result in the depletion of vitamins such as B-complex and minerals like zinc, calcium, iron, and magnesium. These nutrient loses can then starve the sex glands and impair their functions.

Marijuana affects the action of the heart by speeding up its beat as well as creating an irregular beat. **It also reduces the body's immune system response, leaving the user more susceptible to infections (including sexual), colds, and other germs or viruses.** This drug also reduces muscular coordination, resulting in slow reaction time.

Studies suggest that in young men marijuana reduces the testosterone sex hormone level and sperm count after

89

approximately six weeks of use. Marijuana could lead to temporary sterility and even impotency in chronic users. Special dangers for women, exist due to marijuana's frequent contamination with pesticides as well as "hard" drugs such as heroin which could effect estrogen levels, menstrual cycles, and fertility.

COCAINE

"Coke, it's the real thing" is apparently a slogan of an estimated half of all high school students in the United States. Hopefully, many try this dangerous drug only once for curiosities sake.

Even though the cost of cocaine is much higher than marijuana, the effects of the drug must be also. This drug makes the user feel "young, energetic, and confident." In order for a drug to produce such extreme physiological changes, the entire body must be involved. **The brain, liver, heart, nervous system, kidneys, pancreas, and all the hormone producing glands of the body are artificially stimulated in the greatest robbery since the Brinks.** Vitamins A, B, C, D, E, and F as well as all of the minerals are used up at an alarming rate. Frequent users (several times a week) can expect to age very quickly. The drug is so addictive that frequent users don't sleep for days "on it" and will eat very infrequently, if at all. Starvation and malnutrition are eventually the result.

It is not uncommon to see cocaine users after five years either dead, going prematurely grey, becoming impotent, and/or having that "worn-out feeling."

Cocaine is a thief of the immune system and opens a user to many possible infections and diseases later in life.

ALCOHOL

Alcohol depletes the body's supply of vitamin B and minerals, disrupts carbohydrate metabolism, and produces symptoms of dizziness, anxiety, and headaches. **Alcohol is toxic to the liver's ability to metabolize hormones, causing elevated estrogen levels.**

What we drink is **ethyl** alcohol, or **ethamol**. Ethamol is what is left after fermentation of grains, fruits, and vegetable sugar. Carbohydrates and fats can be digested and utilized, but alcohol is essentially foreign to the body. Since it is impossible for the normal process of food digestion to accommodate ethanol, the liver must oxidize it. **The fact that the liver is the only organ that contains the enzymes necessary for dealing with alcohol, explains alcohol's deteriorating effect on the liver.** Another of the liver's responsibilities is the detoxification of drugs and foreign substances of which alcohol is both.

Alcohol's calories are "empty calories" totally devoid of nutritive proteins, minerals, or vitamins. Twelve ounces of beer contain 148 calories; a 3.5 fluid ounce glass of wine contains 94 calories; and one fluid ounce of spirits such as whiskey, vodka, or rum, 70 calories. Drinking a six-pak of beer a day adds up to 324,120 calories per year (3500 excess calories equal one pound).

Alcohol causes inflammation of the stomach, pancreas and intestines, impairing the digestion of food and absorption of nutrients into the blood. It directly encourages malnutrition. Alcohol converts into acetalldehyde, which can interfere with the activation of Vitamin A, Vitamin C and all the B-vitamins by liver cells. **Malnutrition, caused by alcohol consumption, starves the sex glands and their secretion of hormones.**

Alcohol, due to its high simple sugar content, contributes to low blood sugar or hypoglycemia (low blood sugar), causing brain fatigue, headaches, fatigue, memory loss, and severe irritability. Low blood sugar depletes energy, especially sexual energy, leaving a person very tired often to the point of exhaustion.

As an irritant, alcohol destroys healthy tissues, especially those of the brain and sex glands. **Alcohol has been used as an anesthetic because of its ability to deaden the nerves.**

Alcohols's use, other than in extreme moderation, can eventually deaden nerves and senses and weaken glands to the point that sex is either impossible or unfulfilling. **Overconsumption of alcohol can cause impotence (the male can't achieve or maintain an erection), and even causes a lower sperm count (sterility).** The high sugar content can cause sugar cravings, especially during menstruation.

Alcohol depletes body stores of calcium, magnesium, potassium, and in particular, zinc. **The zinc depletion may be the cause of alcohol's profound effects on male impotence.**

Dry, white wines and natural, light beers do have lower amounts of sugar and some nutritional value. Hard liquor, however, has an extreme concentration of alcohol and is not recommended if high-energy sex is your goal. Use alcohol with great care and moderation.

WARNING

Since alcohol is a sedative and contributes to starvation of the sex glands, it is not recommended for those who want to enjoy sex. **Men who drink are poor lovers. Their potency seldom equals their appetite for sex. Habitual use of alcohol poisons the genital organs and can bring about sterility and total atrophy of the reproduction system.**

ALCOHOL AND BIRTH DEFECTS

The March of Dimes warns all pregnant women not to drink alcohol. Even as few as two drinks a week in some women can cause **birth defects.** The March of Dimes states that "alcohol could leave a hangover that could last a lifetime!" Take no chances with your baby; **don't drink.**

SMOKING

Cigarette smoke damages the lungs, air passages, and mucous membranes, resulting in inflammation, irritation, and excess mucus. It can increase your chances of contracting chronic bronchitis, emphysema, and cancer. The types of cancer in which smoking is implicated are lung, mouth, larynx, esophagus, pancreas, kidney, and bladder.

Smoking elevates the blood pressure and increases the cholesterol levels of the blood. People who smoke are at greater risk of heart attacks than those who don't.

Since smoking robs the body of zinc and Vitamin C (one cigarette burns up 25mg of Vitamin C), women are increasing the chances of developing osteoporosis, which studies implicate with smoking women.

Clinical research suggests that tobacco smoking has an adverse effect on sexual urges and could even cause impotency. **Perhaps as with alcohol, the depletion of zinc, so necessary for sexual health in men, is the culprit. Studies indicate that potency is restored when men quit smoking. Toxic substances like nicotine and carbon monoxide in cigarette smoke have a disturbing effect on the sex hormone producing chemistry of the body.**

Women who smoke age much faster than their non-smoking counterparts.

There is no question that smoking is a health hazard. Many organizations, including the March of Dimes and American Cancer Society, warn pregnant women of the dangers of birth defects caused by smoking.

Over 300,000 people die each year from the effects of smoking and millions of other people's health is effected also, according to the Heart Association.

To a non-smoker, smoking is neither sexy nor romantic. In fact, for a non-smoker, kissing a smoker is like **kissing an ashtray**! The stench of the stale smoke lingers in your clothes, on your skin, and in your hair. It is not sexy for men to see a cigarette hanging out of a woman's mouth.

Smoking is not cool, sexy, or virile. When you stop this deadly habit, your attractiveness to the opposite sex will dramatically improve.

Eating the **OH! YES! diet** and exercising regularly will strengthen your nerves, improve your energy, and calm you down, making quitting this unsexy habit easier.

93

CAFFEINE

Caffeine products include coffee, tea, chocolate, colas, and other soft drinks, aspirin, and many other over-the-counter drugs.

Caffeine Sources

Source	Caffeine (mg)
Brewed coffee (1 cup)	85
Instant coffee (1 cup)	60
Brewed black tea (1 cup)	50
Brewed green tea (1 cup)	30
Instant tea (1 cup)	30
Decaffeinated coffee	3
Cola beverage (12 oz.)	32-65
Aspirin compound (pill containing aspirin, phenacetin, and caffeine)	32
Cope, Midol, etc.	32
Excedrin, Anacin (tablet)	60
Pre-Mens	66
Many cold preparations	30
Many stimulants	100
Cocoa (1 cup)	6-42
No Doz (tablet) or Vivarin	100-200

Adapted from P.E. Stephenson, Physiologic and psychotropic effects of caffeine on man, Journal of the American Dietetic Association 71 (1977): 240-247.

Caffeine is a stimulant drug, increasing heart rate and respiration, raising blood pressure, and stimulating the secretion of hormones. Its stimulant effect reaches the maximum one hour after taking. An overdose of caffeine, which varies with the individual, causes dizziness, agitation, irritability, restlessness, frequent headaches, and sleep difficulties. Because caffeine causes extra heart beats and increased blood pressure, it may cause heart attacks in people with damaged hearts.

Caffeine stimulates the adrenal glands to produce more adrenalin and neoadrenalin and continual use will result in depletion and exhaustion of these glands. **Caffeine also is a powerful stimulant to the nervous system and can damage the nerves, liver, kidneys, adrenals, and sex glands.**

Caffeine can cause breast tenderness and relief of such pain is noted when caffeine containing beverages are discontinued. Research implicates caffeine in **fibrocystic disease**, a painful swelling of the breast. Caffeine has been linked to **benign breast lumps and cancer of the pancreas.**

In 1980 the FDA (Food and Drug Administration) advised pregnant women to minimize their caffeine intake because evidence implicates it as a cause of **birth defects.** The ulcer patient or someone with over-acidity of the stomach is advised against caffeine consumption because caffeine stimulates the secretion of stomach acid.

Caffeine is bitter to the taste and is high in oxalic acid, a strong acid, which can burn holes in the stomach lining. Since caffeine is very acidic, calcium and magnesium, which are buffers of acid in the human body, are depleted in order to neutralize the acid effects of caffeine. Heavy coffee drinkers are known to be prone to the development of kidney stones. Kidney stones are made up of oxalic acid and calcium (calcium oxalate) or oxalic acid and magnesium (magnesium oxalate). Coffee, not calcium, is the culprit in the formation of these painful kidney stones. De-caffeinated coffee, low in caffeine, is still high in oxalic acid. Most commercially de-caffeinated coffees have the caffeine extracted with a form of formaldehyde which is carcinogenic (cancer promoting). **Recent studies indicate that women who drink two cups of coffee (either de-caf or regular) have nine times higher rates of breast tumors and cancers then do women who do not drink coffee.**

Caffeine also causes mood swings and depletes the body's stores of B-complex, thus interfering with sex gland operation and carbohydrate metabolism. **In addition, caffeine depletes such essential minerals for sex gland and hormone production as iron and potassium.** Caffeine can interfere with the kidney's function, causing water retention and swelling.

Caffeine containing foods such as coffee, cola, and chocolate provide quick energy but provide few nutrients and can disrupt hormonal chemistry. If you eat the **OH! YES! diet** and exercise regularly, you will not need a caffeine "fix" for energy.

It is very important to remember that the elimination of coffee and tea while continuing the use of colas, soft drinks, chocolate, and candy **does little** to reduce the harmful and hazardous effects of caffeine on the sex glands and sex hormones.

WARNING

Researchers have known for some time that tea and coffee reduce iron absorption by as much as 87% when drank with a meal. In the U.S. where "iron-poor" blood is prevalent in premenopausal women because of menstrual blood losses, tea and coffee are not advised.

Although the carbonation of caffeine in soft drinks neutralizes the oxalic acid effect and many cola drinks are chemically de-caffeinated, other hazards exist in soft drinks.

Nearly all soft drinks contain phosphoric acid, a form of phosphorous which upsets the natural balance of phosphorous and calcium in your body. **Significant use of soft drinks containing phosphoric acid will deplete calcium reserves, possibly leading to menstrual cramping, irregular menstruation, thyroid depletion, insomnia, and even weight gain.** The continuous use of diet sodas could actually upset the hormonal balance, particularly of the thyroid and sex glands, causing a sluggish metabolism which might result in weight gain and diminished sexual function.

Substitutes for Caffeine

Coffee Substitutes—Cafix, Pero, and Postum

Tea Substitutes—Herbal teas (herbs are medicine and not to be used continually)

Colas and Soft Drinks—In transition use colas that do not contain phospheric acid or caffeine, unsweetened fruit juices, and water. Water is much better than soft drinks for those trying to lose weight.

Chocolate—Carob, a bean, is totally free of caffeine and has 70% less fat in it, unless palm kernel oil is added.

Aspirin—A 500mg calcium tablet will relax the nerves, thereby relieving tension headaches.

THE PERSON WHO WISHES TO BE SEXUALLY ACTIVE INTO ADVANCED AGE WILL SAY *NO* TO DRUGS.

5

Sexy Foods: The OH! YES! Diet!

"In our selection of food, we are already committing ourselves to health or disease."

—GST

When I was a little boy, I wanted to be a professional baseball player; catcher was my position. My hero was Yogi Berra, catcher for the New York Yankees. I wore my Little League uniform just like Yogi did, threw the ball like he did, batted the way he did, and my number was eight, just like his. Why did I do these things! **I was emulating the best, the most successful**, catcher in the major leagues at that time. Yogi Berra was a winner! **If I wanted to be successful, the odds were pretty good that if I would follow a winner, I could be a winner, too.** I certainly wouldn't follow a failure or a loser would I?

If you want to be healthy, energetic, and sexually active throughout your life, doesn't it seem logical to study people or cultures renowned for their superior health longevity and sexual vitality. People who are virtually free of cancer, heart disease, strokes, diabetes, and arthritis; men who father children at the age of a hundred years or more. These virile people are our examples of the "winners" in the health game. **But health is not a game, it is a matter of life and death.** Such cultures and lifestyles, proven to promote health, vitality, and longevity, should be the standard of health for all nutritionists, doctors, nurses, dieticians, not to mention anyone who is interested in his or her own health.

Much of the confusion and misinformation in nutrition literature would end if more practitioners in the field studied health in the way of Dr. Paavo Airola and Dr. Bernard Jensen. Both of these doctors traveled worldwide to study cultures renowned for their superior health and longevity. Such cultures include the traditional Japanese, the Vilcabambas of Ecuador, the Hunza people of Kashmir, the traditional Bulgarians, the Abkhazians of Russia, and the Yucatan and Chihuahua Indians of Mexico. People living in these extraordinary cultures live an average of 85 years, and many live to be over a hundred, with very little degenerative disease. In their old age, people simply go to sleep one night and don't wake up the next morning. Few people die a "natural" death in America anymore; instead we suffer greatly and die prematurely.

Healthy Cultures

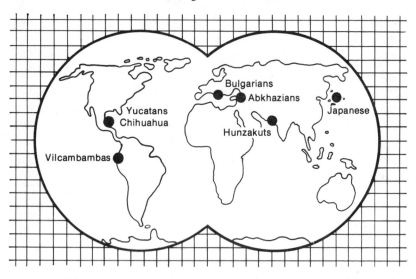

Individuals in healthy cultures have developed a lifestyle permitting full, energetic lives and natural deaths. Although scattered throughout the world, these cultures have strikingly similar eating and living habits. The following guidelines are a proven eating pattern which has kept people well for generations, and since these people exhibit sexual virility and energy even past a hundred years of age, I call their formula for a fertile, virile, and energetic life the **"Optimum Health for Youth, Energy and Sex,"** or the OH! YES! Diet.

OH! YES! DIET

FOOD	% OF DIET
1. Grains, Beans, Seeds, Nuts............	50%
2. Vegetables	30%
3. Fruits	10%
4. Dairy Products	6%
5. Meat (fish, fowl, beef, pork, lamb)	4%

FOOD GROUP	% OF DIET
1. Complex Carbohydrates	70-75%
2. Fats.............................	15-20%
3. Protein	10%

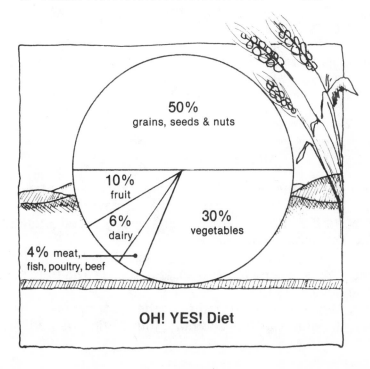

OH! YES! Diet

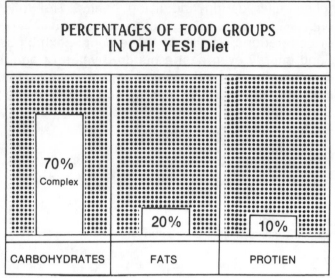

PERCENTAGES OF FOOD GROUPS
IN OH! YES! Diet

70%
Complex

20%

10%

CARBOHYDRATES | FATS | PROTIEN

Source: U.S. Department of Agriculture - Agriculture Research
Service.

The Standard American Diet (S.A.D.) has a very poor track record, as high rates of PMS, prostitis, infertility, impotency, hormonal imbalances, as well as heart disease, diabetes and cancer among Americans abound.

IMPORTANCE OF SEEDS

All life on the planet Earth comes from **seed**. Sperm, a form of seed, is vital to the creation of new life. A woman may be fertile, but if the man hasn't enough seed (sterility), she will be unable to conceive.

So it is in the plant kingdom also that all plant food, grains, beans, seeds, vegetables, and fruits grown from seed or sperm-like substance.

If we examine the structure of the most **potent** of plant seeds, the grains, seeds and nuts, four distinctive parts are found:

1. The **husk, shell, or hull**, a protective covering with little nutritional value.
2. The **bran**, primarily insoluble fiber called cellulose, containing small amounts of B vitamins, minerals, especially iron, and protein.
3. The **endosperm**, constituting the largest part of the grain, is mostly starch, incomplete protein and trace amounts of nutrients.
4. The **germ** is the center, embryo, or heart of the grain, seed, or nut, and is especially rich in B vitamins, Vitamin E, protein, unsaturated fat, minerals, and carbohydrates.

Hidden deep within the seed is the **germ**, where an abundance of vitamins and minerals necessary for endocrine gland nourishment and subsequent production of sex hormones is found. A virtual **treasure chest of vitality and energy, the grains, seeds and nuts have no equal in the food kingdom.**

The starch or **endosperm** portion of the grain is a pure source of energy or carbohydrate called **glucose**. This pure energy feeds the seed during its incubation period and early growth in the soil, until it can begin to assimilate the nutrients from the soil. **The bran and the germ of the seed, rich in B vitamins and minerals assist in the digestion or utilization of the starch in the endosperm.** Grains, beans, seeds, and nuts also contain the genetic information in order to reproduce after their own kind. For instance, contained in very kernel of corn is the ability to reproduce **thousands** of kernels of corn from a single seed. How magnificent and powerful is this energy packed into a plant seed. **All life on this Earth either eats the plants grown from these tiny seeds or eats the animals who have eaten the plants of these powerful seeds.**

MAKE-UP OF A KERNEL OF GRAIN
Oats, brown rice, millet, barley, buckwheat, rye, cornmeal.

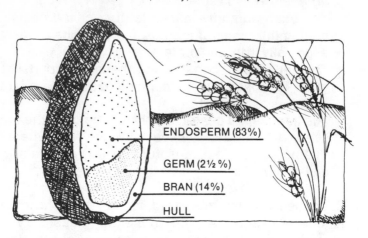

ENDOSPERM (83%)

GERM (2½%)

BRAN (14%)

HULL

TOTAL NUTRIENTS IN A KERNEL OF GRAIN

GERM	BRAN	ENDOSPERM
Thiamine (B¹)	Pyridoxine (B⁶)	Starch
Riboflavin (B²)	Panthothenic Acid	Traces of
Pyridoxine (B⁶)	(B⁵)	Vitamins &
Protein	Riboflavin (B²)	Minerals
Pantothenic Acid	Thiamine (B¹)	
(B⁵)	Protein	
Niacin (B³)		
Vitamin E		

MINERALS

Calcium	Sulphur	Barium
Iron	Iodine	Silver
Phosophorus	Fluorine	Inositol
Magnesium	Chlorine	Folic Acid
Potassium	Sodium	Choline
Manganese	Silicon	And other trace
Copper	Boron	materials

Source: Nutrition Almanac

In the whole unprocessed seeds of grain, seeds, and nuts, we find abundant minerals like phosphorus, calcium, magnesium, zinc, copper, iron, potassium, and minerals especially important to the sex glands. Grains, beans, seeds, and nuts are excellent sources of the B vitamins, Vitamin E, and Vitamin F, the unsaturated fatty acids. These vitamins help produce hormones vital to sexual energy.

Protein, complete with all the amino acids, is present in the seeds. Protein needed to produce sex hormones and enzymes for optimum health and longevity.

COMPLETE PROTEIN IN SEEDS

Protein is found in both plants and animals. Protein consists of 22 amino acids connected in chains. The length and sequence of the amino acid chains distinguish one type of protein from another. Of the 22 amino acids, nine cannot be produced within the body (called essential amino acids) and must therefore be included in your diet. These nine amino acids are: trypotophane, histine, phenylalanine, leucine, isoleucine, valine, lysine, threonine, and methionine. Eggs are considered the only food which has the "ideal" balance of essential amino acids needed by humans. The egg is the reference point or standard against which all other proteins are measured. **Although vegetable proteins compared with egg protein are lower in quantity of essential amino acids, they are not missing any of them.** The real standard of protein is its quantity. Quality refers to the amino acids' usability by the human body. If vegetable and animal proteins are considered in terms of quality, there is little difference between the two classes of proteins. Since most of the healthy cultures use little or no animal protein in their diets and have no amino acid deficiencies, perhaps the egg, "the ideal reference protein," contains amino acids in excess of human requirements. **Although an egg may be the Rolls-Royce of proteins, vegetable proteins provide more than adequate essential amino acids to maintain optimum health.**

ESSENTIAL AMINO ACID CONTENT per 100 grams (3½ oz.)

	TRYPTO-PHAN	THREO-NINE	ISOLEU-CINE	LEU-CINE	LYSINE	METH-IONINE	PHENY-LALANINE	VALINE	HISTI-DINE	PROTEIN GRAMS
GRAINS										
BARLEY	160	433	545	889	433	184	661	643	239	8.2
CORN (field whl)	61	398	462	1,296	288	186	454	510	206	8.9
MILLET	248	456	635	1,746	383	270	506	682	240	9.9
RICE, brown	81	294	352	646	296	135	377	524	126	7.5
RYE, whl grain	137	448	515	813	494	191	571	631	276	12.1
LEGUMES										
PINTO BEANS	213	997	1,306	1,976	1,708	232	1,270	1,395	655	22.9
LENTILS	216	896	1,316	1,760	1,528	180	1,104	1,360	548	24.7
NUTS/SEEDS										
ALMONDS	176	610	873	1,454	582	259	1,146	1,124	514	18.6
PECANS	138	389	553	773	435	153	564	525	273	9.2
SUNFLOWER	343	911	1,276	1,736	868	443	1,220	1,354	586	24.0

in milligrams

Source: Amino Acid Content of Foods, Home Economics Research Report #4, U.S. Department of Agriculture, 1968.

Since most complex carbohydrates contain all the essential amino acids, complimentary protein meals to approximate the ideal pattern of amino acids in an egg is unnecessary.

The plants from seeds are called carbohydrates and include:

1. Grains
2. Beans
3. Seeds
4. Nuts
5. Vegetables
6. Fruits

DEVELOPMENT OF AGRICULTURE

The history of humankind is the story of man's transition from nomadic hunting to establishing settlements and growing his own food (agriculture). People who had wandered in search of food began to plant it instead and remained in one place long enough to harvest their crops. The beginning of agriculture marked the beginning of civilization since our ancestors had time (no longer spending all of their time looking for food) to build cities and establish systems of thought and art.

Farming and agriculture have developed domesticated

cereal grains, vegetables, and fruits thousands of years ago that remain in use to this day. Human beings have lived **primarily** on complex carbohydrates for thousands of years. Anthropologists have established the length of time some of these grain have been on Earth.

> Rice — 12,000 years
> Beans, Squash — 9,000 years
> Wheat, Barley — 7,000 years
> Refined Sugar — 100 years

Other than tomatoes and coffee, no important new plants have been cultivated in the last two thousand years.

CARBOHYDRATES: IDEAL ENERGY

Carbohydrates in the form of starch are the ideal source of human energy and fuel for most bodily functions, including the brain, nerves, and muscles and consequently for our sex glands and hormones as well.

As a growing child, I was taught that protein, not carbohydrates, was the best source of energy for my body. I accepted the following equation:

$$Energy = Protein$$
$$Protein = Meat \qquad (WRONG)$$
$$Energy = Meat$$

Actually, the body's source of energy is **glucose**, not protein. Protein can be converted into glucose but only in the absence of adequate carbohydrates will the body **devalue** protein for immediate energy use. **Carbohydrates are designed for immediate energy requirements.** Carbohyrates break down into glucose most readily of all foods. The correct energy equation is:

$$Energy = Glucose$$
$$Glucose = Carbohydrates \qquad (RIGHT)$$
$$Energy = Carbohydrates$$

Carbohydrates provide the needed glucose for energy of your body and without an abundance of them in your diet there will not be sufficient energy for sex.

Besides containing glucose that translates into vitality and energy, carbohydrates particularly grains have the vitamins and minerals needed for optimal operation of the brain, nervous system, immune system and endocrine glands.

Regular eating of grains, beans, and legumes are essential for anyone wanting sexual vitality throughout life. Because of their prime importance, we will take a detailed look at the history of the most beneficial of these, their nutrient content, and the relationship of these nutrients to your sexual energy. I've also included a few recipes using each of the grains, beans, and legumes.

WHAT TO EAT FOR SEXUAL VITALITY

BARLEY

Barley is one of the oldest cultivated cereals and probably originated in Africa and Asia. The Egyptians used this valuable food for man and animals as early as 5000 B.C. and in China about 3000 B.C. It was the chief bread plant of the Hebrews, Greeks, and the Romans. Barley is mentioned frequently in the Bible and many of the prophets ate it as their staple food.

Barley was grown in Europe in the Middle Ages and brought to America by the British and the Dutch. It is an excellent source of complete protein (contains all eight essential amino acids), natural sugars, high energy starch, some fat, and is rich in calcium, iron, thiamin (B_1), riboflavin (B_2), and niacin (B_3).

The spread of barley to the West was not for food but rather for making beer. Beer is brewed from barley germinated into malt (malt liquor). Barley, like most grains, when fermented, develops very sweet sugars, a testimony to the ability of brains to break down into glucose or sugar in your body.

Less than one-tenth of the barley grown in the U.S. is used for human food, and the processed pearled barley with the protein removed in the milling process is the primary barley sold. Natural brown barley (hulled but not pearled) can be found in natural food stores. Even pearled barley is better than no barley.

Barley is hearty and filling when added to soups and stews. It can also be used in place of rice in any dish and can be used as flour in pancakes.

COOKED BARLEY

Cook ¼ cup barley in 6 cups water for 2 to 4 hours. Strain and add to soups.

1 cup coarsely cracked barley, soaked overnight
2 cups water

Bring water to boil, add soaked barley, cover, and cook over low heat for ten minutes. Can be eaten as a breakfast cereal along with added apple juice or other sweetener and fruit.

MUSHROOM-BARLEY SOUP

1 pound mushrooms, sliced
2 cups barley (soak 12 hours before cooking)
1 diced onion
*Quick Sip and Vegetable broth to taste
2 cloves garlic

Place ingredients in crockpot. Cover with distilled water or spring water and cook overnight on "low" setting.

BUCKWHEAT

Buckwheat is not wheat! It is not tall and straight but

branching and weedlike, with heart-shaped leaves and white flowers that attract hungry bees.

Buckwheat was used by the Phoenicians in ancient China and introduced into Eastern Europe and the Mediterranean by tribes migrating from Siberia and Manchuria.

Buckwheat is an extremely nutritious cereal containing complete protein, vitamins, and minerals, especially manganese and magnesium (important sex hormone production). It is high in **rutin**, a bioflavinoid, found to be helpful in lowering blood pressure as well as having a beneficial effect on the whole circulatory system.

Buckwheat is one of those foods which you either love or hate. The Jewish people eat a traditional buckwheat dish called Kasha.

KASHA

   1 cup toasted buckwheat groats
   1 egg, beaten
    2 cups water or chicken broth stock

Add buckwheat groats and egg into boiling water or stock and cook over low heat for 15 to 20 minutes.

Add butter or olive oil to finished product and serve as a side dish.

*Add Vegit, Quick Sip or Jensen's Vegetable Broth to taste.

   Quick Sip (soy sauce without the salt), Vegit, and Jensen's Vegetable Broth Powder are available at health food stores.

BUCKWHEAT PANCAKES

1 cup buckwheat flour
½ cup oat flour
2 eggs
2 cups buttermilk, yogurt or kefir

Mix flour and buttermilk or other curdled milk and blend well. If batter is too thick, add water. Fry on lightly buttered or sesame oiled griddle on low heat.

Serve with butter and/or unsweetened apple sauce topping.

CORN (MAIZE)

According to archaeologists, corn grew wild in southern Mexico nine thousand years ago. The Indians of South and Central America have been using maize or corn for centuries. The Mayas, Incas, and Aztecs worshipped the plant as a god when they called it Cinteotl. The American Indians thought so highly of the grain that it became a part of their religious practices. **The American Indians called corn, "Seed of Seeds," "Sacred Mother," and "Blessed Daughter."**

Corn is very economical since it yields three times as much harvest per acre as wheat.

CHIEF VARIETIES

Flint Corn—very hardy, shiny grain with percentage of protein content.

Dent Corn—more starchy than flint and this variety predominates U.S. "corn belt."

Flown Corn—usually white and starch is so soft that it easily forms a paste when mixed with water.

Sweet Corn—a variety of yellow grain referred to as "Indian Corn" or "corn on the cob."

Popcorn—the popping action turns the grain inside out. When the water contained in the center of the grain is heated, it builds up such pressure that it explodes.

Yellow corn is preferable since it has a larger amount of Vitamin A, while the white varieties have only negligible amounts. Yellow corn contains a larger amount of starch with the germ particularly rich in unsaturated fatty acids.

Corn is not particularly rich in minerals or B vitamins. Corn is best eaten with beans to increase its nutritive value. To yield one tablespoon of corn oil requires twelve ears of corn and all of the fiber and most of the nutrients are removed in the process. When buying corn tortillas in the supermarket, look for the varieties **without salt.**

CORNMEAL MUSH

1 cup whole cornmeal
1 cup cold watr
4 cups boiling water

Stir cornmeal into cold water. Pour boiling water into the top of a double boiler and slowly stir cornmeal mixture into boiling water. Place double boiler pan over water and cook mush, covered, 20-25 minutes. Stir frequently. Add fruit such as bananas and currants. Dr. Jensen's Apple Juice Concentrate or barley malt syrup are good sweetener additions.

MILLET

Millet has the distinction among grains of being able to support human life in the absence of all other food. It takes its name from the Latin word meaning "a thousand" because of its prolific seeds and its fertility. This grain has been found in the pyramids and tombs of the ancient Egyptians. Native to eastern Asia, held sacred by the Chinese, it is a staple of northern China today. Over 2,500 years ago Pythagoras, the

Greek philosopher, encouraged his followers to eat millet to improve their health and vitality. In Ezekiel, Chapter 4, Ezekiel was told by God to make bread out of millet and other grains. **Millet is the staple food of the Hunzakuts, a culture renowned for their superior health, virility, and long life (many lived over a hundred years).**

Unfortunately, millet is used mainly for birdseed in the United States, though millions of people eat it daily in Asia and Africa. **Also, the Georgian people of Russia—another long-living group reported to be free of heart disease, cancer, and arthritis—eat millet regularly.**

Millet has all the essential amino acids in percentages comparable to meat or dairy products. It contains all the essential minerals and is especially rich in calcium and magnesium (needed for hormone production), along with abundant amounts of potassium, iron, and florine. The choline in millet helps to keep cholesterol levels under control. Millet is rich in thiamine (B_1), riboflavin (B_2), as well as Vitamin A and Vitamin C. It is an alkaline food, unlike other grains, and can be well tolerated by individuals with over-acid and ulcerative conditions as well as by rheumatism, arthritis, and diabetes sufferers. Millet, according to Dr. Paavo Airola, is non-fattening because of its alkaline-forming properties. Alkalines tend to dissolve and counteract fat building.

Millet is an easily digestive, high fiber grain producing carbohydrate of the highest quality, building vitality and virility.

TOMATO MILLET

    3 cups cooked whole millet
    1 medium onion, chopped
    1 clove garlic, chopped
    4 large tomatoes
    1 cup water
    1 cup cooked, dried, lima beans
    2 tsp basil
    2 tablespoons fresh parsley, chopped

Place tomatoes and water in a blender, blend until smooth. Combine ingredients in 1½ quart baking dish, bake for 1 hour at 350° F.

MILLET DELIGHT

1½ cups water
½ cup millet
½ dried avocado or 1 tablespoon Olive Oil
1 tomato, diced
Quick Sip to taste

Boil water and add millet, cover, simmer for 20 minutes. (Check water and add as needed.) Millet should be fluffy, but not mushy or soggy. Add diced avocado, diced tomato, and seasoning before serving.

OATS

Unfortunately, like millet, oats are most widely used in the United States as animal food. Oats are also excellent human food, as the Scottish people have known for centuries. This grain was developed around 2500 B.C. in northern Africa, the Near East and Russia. Oats also found their way to Europe and Britain and became a dietary staple in Scotland, Ireland, and northern England.

Oats are milled by first removing the husks and then the inner grain or groat is cleaned very thoroughly. An oat groat (the whole grain) is very soft and can be easily crushed flat by rolling a rolling pin over its surface. Breaking down the grain in this manner, thereby exposing more of its surface, makes it easier to cook than in its groat form. Commercially rolled oats—old fashioned, not quick—are just as nutritious as those done at home. Oatflakes are a popular ingredient in many health products available in grocery and health food stores. Oat flour is an excellent ingredient in home-made breads and are now available in health food stores.

Many beauty aids contain oats, such as an oatmeal and

vinegar face mask. Oats are an excellent source of oat bran, a high fiber and therefore oats are beneficial to constipation, unless the rolled oats are over-cooked and become like glue.

Oats are a good source of B vitamins, protein, and fiber. **People, as well as horses, will develop endurance and strength by eating them regularly.**

OUTSTANDING OAT BREAKFAST

½ cup old-fashioned rolled oats
2 tablespoons currants
1 banana
2 tablespoons yogurt (optional)
½ grated apple (optional)
10 almonds (whole or ground)

Pour boiling water over rolled oats and currants until water is ½ inch above oats, cover and steam for 5 minutes. Pour off water and add remaining ingredients.

GRANOLA

6 cups rolled oats
1 cup shredded coconut
½ cup sunflower seeds
¼ cup sesame seeds
¼ cup chopped almonds
1 cup raisins
¼ cup barley malt syrup
1 teaspoon vanilla
¼ cup water

Combine oats, coconut, seeds, and nuts in a large bowl. In a separate pan mix barley malt syrup, water, and vanilla. Stir over low heat until smooth. Pour over grains, mixing thoroughly. Spread mixture thinly on cookie sheets and bake at 250° for 30-45 minutes, stirring frequently. Oats should be crisp, but coconut should not be burned. Uncooked is best.

Add raisins and place in airtight container in refrigerator.

Use as a snack like popcorn or add fruit and yogurt for breakfast.

RICE

Rice has been a staple food of Asians and Orientals since 3000 B.C. **In fact, it is the staple food crop of over half the world's people and approximately 200 billion pounds of rice are produced in the world each year.** Rice was first cultivated in India, and Buddhism was the factor which spread the cultivated rice through China, Japan, and Asia. In the U.S. we grow one percent of the world crop and eat only a fraction of that small percentage. The average Oriental eats 400 pounds of rice a year, while most Americans eat less than 10 pounds a year.

During most of the year, rice plants must be under from one to eight inches of water, then the fields are drained, and the grain is picked. In its natural brown state, rice contains about .8 percent protein, two percent oil, 78 percent carbohydrates along with calcium, iron, zinc, and most of the B vitamins. After the husk, bran, and germ are removed by milling, a white, starchy, denatured food remains. Beri-beri is the deficiency disease associated with those who subsist on a diet of polished rice (after the third polishing the thiamine, the deficiency of which causes beri-beri, is totally lost). Brown rice, which has two major varieties, short or long, has only the husk or hull removed, thereby leaving the nutrients intact. Ironically, only the poorest people in the East eat brown rice while it is status symbol to have the white, polished type.

Rice flour can be added to bread recipes in place of wheat flour. This is especially important for those who are allergic to wheat. Brown rice takes longer than polished white rice to cook, but it hardly ever is gummy like white rice can become. **Rice can be added to soups, stews, or even as a side dish.**

BASIC BROWN RICE

1 cup brown rice (long grain is less starchy)
2 cups water or stock

Bring water to boil, add rice, simmer for 45 minutes. Check after a half hour and add ¼ cup water if rice seems dry. When done, add butter and Quick Sip to taste.

SAFFRON RICE

(Basis of many Middle Eastern dishes)

1 tablespoon butter or olive oil
1 cup uncooked brown rice
2 cups vegetable or chicken stock
¼ tsp powdered saffron
1 tablespoon Vegit

Saute rice until translucent. Add other ingredients and place in a covered pot. Cook over low heat for one hour. Serve with fish, chicken, or other cooked vegetables.

SPANISH TOMATO RICE

In a 10" skillet combine:

3 tablespoons Olive Oil
1 cup chopped onion
¼ cup chopped green peppers

Cook until tender but not brown. Add:

3 large tomatoes, pureed
1 cup water
¾ cup of uncooked long-grain rice
½ cup Mexican Hot Sauce

Cover and simmer 35 to 40 minutes. Serves six.

MEXICAN FIESTA TOSTADA

2 cups pinto beans (soaked 12 hours)
Boil for 4-5 hours or until done. Add one large diced onion and 2 large cloves of diced garlic. When beans are done, whip mixture until smooth. Put beans on corn tortilla. *Garnish with chopped lettuce and tomatoes. Add Mexican hot sauce and guacamole if desired.

*Bake tortilla for five minutes in oven or until crisp.

MEXICAN HOT SAUCE

6 large tomatoes blended
2 8 oz. jars tomato sauce (salt free)
3 diced green chiles
2 diced jalapenos
1 large onion, diced
4 large cloves garlic, diced
1 tbsp. red chili powder
1 tbsp. ground cumin
1 tsp. ground oregano
1 cup water

Bring to a boil; simmer for 15 minutes. Yields two quarts.

WOK VEGGIES AND RICE

2 cups water
1 cup brown rice
1 large carrot, sliced
½ leek or onion, diced
⅓ pound of firm Tofu or chicken (optional)
1 cup kale, broccoli or cauliflower (cut up)

Cook basic brown rice (millet may be substituted) 15 minutes before rice is done, saute cut vegetables in olive oil in a pan or wok until tender. Add rice and continue mixing well for a few minutes. Add Quick Sip to taste.

DRIED PEAS AND BEANS

Dried peas and beans have long been used as a food staple in healthy cultures and can contribute to your sexual health.

Beans, peas, and lentils are all fruits of leguminous plants found within pods. Legumes which sometimes are also called pulses, have been eaten for thousands of years. They were cultivated in the Tigria-Euphrates Valley nearly four thousand years ago and are referred to in the Bible.

Pureed lentils or split peas are called dal, in India, are high in protein, and have been eaten regularly in the East Indian diet for thousands of years. Pureed chick-peas or garbanzo beans have been a staple in Arab and South American countries for centuries.

Regular Bean	Cooker Cooking Time	Pressure Minimum Cooking Time	Cooking Water	Dry Bewans	Cooked Beans
Black beans	1½ hours	20-25 min.	4 cups	1 cup	2 cups
Black-eyed peas	1 hour	20-25 min.	3 cups	1 cup	2 cups
Pinto beans	2½ hours	20-25 min.	3 cups	1 cup	2 cups
Kidney beans	1½ hours	20-25 min.	3 cups	1 cup	2 cups
Soybeans	3 hrs. or more	20-25 min.	3 cups	1 cup	2 cups
Garbanzo beans	3 hours	40-45 min	4 cups	1 cup	4 cups
Lentils & Split peas	1 hour	10-15 min.	3 cups	1 cup	2¼ cups
Great Northern beans	2 hours	20-25 min.	3½ cups	1 cup	2 cups
Navy beans	1½ hours	20-25 min.	3 cups	1 cup	2 cups
Lima beans	1½ hours	20-25 min.	2 cups	1 cup	1¼ cups

*To make less musical grains, all beans and legumes should be soaked **at least** 12 hours, pour off water, add water and cook. Cooking beans and legumes with a piece of kelp or other sea vegetable helps reduce musical quality also.

HUMUS SPREAD

2 cups cooked garbanzo beans
2 tablespoons sesame seed or olive oil
1 tablespoon raw sesame seeds

Mash cooked garbanzos well and stir in oil to the consistency of a spread. Blend in sesame seeds. Can be stored in jars in refrigerator for several days. This spread can be put in pocket-pita bread with lettuce and diced tomatoes to make a quick lunch or after-school snack for hungry children.

LENTIL RICE SOUP

1½ cups lentils
2 cups stock or water
½ cup long grain brown rice
¼ tsp ground cumin
1 medium onion
2 capfuls of Jensen's Quick Sip
1 tablespoon Jensen's Vegetable Broth
1 tablespoon olive oil

Rinse lentils and place in crockpot with stock or water, seasonings, onion, and rice. Cook on "low" for several hours.

BLACK BEANS AND RICE

1 cup dried turtle beans (black beans)
    (soaked for 12 hours)
2 cups water
1 onion, diced
1 clove garlic, chopped
1 tablespoon fresh parsley

Cook beans in water for two hours or until tender. Saute onion, garlic, and parsley in olive or sesame oil until tender.

Add drained black beans and cook until mixed well. Serve with Vegit and Quick Sip. Serve over cooked brown rice.

NUTS

Eat almonds for sexual energy! (See chapter on Aphrodisiacs.) They are the **king** of the nuts!

SEEDS

PUMPKIN SEEDS

Pumpkins are one of the largest of the vegetable varieties. **In China, the pumpkin and its seeds were considered fertility foods, a symbol of health and fruitfulness.** The Chinese called pumpkin, "Emperor of the Gardens" because of its high energy and largeness.

In Greece, the saying, "healthier than a pumpkin," was coined and the Greeks worshipped the Pumpkin Goddess.

The seeds of pumpkins contain 15 percent high-quality protein, 40 percent unsaturated fatty acids and contain high sources of Vitamin E and Vitamin F, all necessary to the optimum functioning of the endocrine glands and their hormones. They are excellent sources of Vitamin A, as well as many of B-Complex family. Pumpkin seeds are extremely high in zinc (40 to 50 parts per million). They are very helpful where additional food sources of zinc and/or copper are needed. The oil of pumpkin seeds can also be purchased and taken in capsule form. Eat them as a snack along with almonds and sunflower seeds.

SESAME SEEDS

According to Hindu mythology, sesame seeds are a symbol of immortality and the Assyrians are said to have drunk sesame wine to gain strength and power to create the world.

Sesame seeds are recorded in the ancient history of China, Japan, Mid-East, and Mediterranean countries. Sesame seeds, ground and mixed with honey, were enjoyed by the Jews and Egyptians for added vitality.

The ancient Greek soldiers carried sesame seeds for emergency energy.

Sesame seed oil is a rich source of polyunsaturated fatty acids, helpful in sex hormone production. The seeds contain lecithin, choline and inositol, important to brain and nervous system operation. Sesame is very rich in calcium, magnesium, and phosphorous, all required for adequate estrogen, progesterone and testosterone production.

The oil of sesame, used for thousands of years by the Japanese in wok cooking, is a clear, bland oil which has the distinction of containing **sesamol**. Sesamol has the property of keeping sesame oil from going rancid and maintaining its fresh, cold-pressed nutrient value.

Open Sesame!

SUNFLOWER SEEDS

The Mayan and Suma Indians* worshipped the sun and revered the sunflower because of its resemblance to their god. Their temples were decorated in pure gold emblems of this flower. The sunflower is a true heliotrope, a plant which turns during the day to follow the path of the sun. The priestesses were also crowned with sunflowers.

Sunflower seeds are a powerhouse of nutrition and sexual energy. They contain all essential amino acids and are rich in polyunsaturated fatty acids. The minerals of iron, copper, magnesium, and potassium. They contain high amounts of B vitamins (higher even than wheat germ). Sunflower seeds have the distinction of being one of the few plants with Vitamin D and also rich amount of Vitamin A, E, F, and K. Sunflowers seeds contain all the fat soluble vitamins needed by the human body, especially the endocrine glands.

They are delicious as a snack. Make certain they are soft, fresh, and not roasted or salted.

WARNING

The fat in nuts and seeds can go rancid! Roasting them will accomplish this unhealthy end. Eat them raw. Refrigerate all nuts and seeds.

FISH

Fish are distinguished by their living habits, there are fresh water, salt water, and shellfish. Shellfish such as shrimp, lobster, crab, snails, and oysters are all **scavenger** fish that "clean-up" the ocean. They are the "rats" of the ocean and not fit for human consumption. **The fin and scale fish are the cleanest and safest to eat**.

From the charts, fish are excellent sources of high-quality protein, low in calories and lower in fat than red meats. They are free from added synthetic hormones and antibiotics and are a good source of polyunsaturated fatty acids.

Fish	Measure	Calories	Protein (g)	Total Fat (g)	Cholesterol (mg)
Bass	1 lb	472	85.7	9.5	0
Cod	1 lb	354	9.8	3.31	227
Haddock	1 lb	358	83.0	2.99	272
Halibut	1 lb	454	94.8	4.98	227
Herring	1 lb	798	78.5	28.1	386
Mackeral	1 lb	566	86.2	44.4	431
Perch	1 lb	451	86.2	11.3	0
Salmon	1 lb	984	102	60.8	272
Snapper	1 lb	422	89.8	5.44	0
Trout	1 lb	885	97.5	51.7	249

*lb = pounds, (g) = grams, (mg) = milligrams
Composition of Foods, U.S. Agriculture Handbook No. 8

Meat	Measure	Calories	Protein (g)	Total Fat (g)	Cholesterol (mg)
Chuck Roast	1 lb	905	78.8	75	270
Club Steak	1 lb	1443	58.9	132	261
Ground Beef	1 lb	1216	81.2	96.2	307
Sirloin Steak	1 lb	1316	71.0	112.0	261
T-Bone Steak	1 lb	1596	59.0	168.0	261
Lamb Chop	1 lb	1146	63.7	97.0	270
Lamb Leg	1 lb	845	67.7	61.7	265
Pork Chop	1 lb	1065	61.0	89.0	260
Bacon	1 lb	3016	38.1	314	999
Ham	1 lb	1535	66.7	138	318
Veal Cutlet	1 lb	681	72.3	41	254
Chicken Breast	1 lb	394	74.5	18	239
Chicken Leg	1 lb	313	51.2	30.7	239
Turkey (light)	1 lb	798	149	37.6	458

---

*lb † pounds, (g) = grams, (mg) = milligrams
Composition of Foods, U.S. Agriculture Handbook No. 8

The fats that all fish contain (5-40%) are called omega-3 fatty acids. Fish are especially rich in two fatty acids, (1) dorosahexaenoic acid (DHA) and (2) eicosapentaenoic acid (EPA). Dr. William Connor of Oregon Health Services in Portland states that strong scientific evidence suggests omega-3 fatty acids can decrease the incidence of coronary heart disease. In several studies, a diet high in fish oils has reduced the incidence of breast and pancreatic* cancers in rats according to the journal of the National Cancer Institute.

The omega-3 oils are excellent sources of polyunsaturated fatty acids necessary in the production of sexual hormones and since scientific data suggests their preventative effect against heart disease and cancer, the author recommends substituting fin and scale fish for other high-protein foods in the diet. In health cultures only six percent of the diet is meat, poultry and fish and therefore, two or three times a week is more than adequate to insure a low fat, low protein diet, rich in the grains, nuts and seeds so vital for increased vitality and virility.

Although chicken and turkey are low in fat relative to red meats, the commercial poultry producers add synthetic hormones and antibiotics in the feed. Poultry **does not** contain the omega-3 oils either.

WARNINGS

Since contaminants can accumulate in fish fat, make certain the fish comes from unpolluted waters. **Salmon is one of the safest fish and the highest in omega-3 fatty acids.** Due to the possibility of bacterial infection, fresh fish can only be kept at room temperature for two hours and when refrigerated, used within two days after being defrosted. Fish should be cooked at a low temperature (300 to 325 degrees) in order to preserve the flavors, juices and nutrients.

Remember that it is the grains, not the high protein foods like fish, which are vital to obtain Optimum Health for Youth, Energy, and Sex (OH! YES!).

OH! YES! DIET FOR SEXUAL VITALITY

GRAINS

Brown rice, rolled oats (no Quick Oats), millet, buckwheat, barley, rye, cornmeal and wheat berries.

BEANS AND LEGUMES

Pinto, black (turtle, not soy), garbanzo, azuki, black-eyed peas, lentils, lima, kidney, split peas. Soy beans are not recommended unless you are of Oriental descent. The trypsin inhibitors (enzyme for proteins) in soy make it indigestible to westerners. **Peanuts, high in fat and acid, are almost indigestible to humans.** For best digestion of peanuts, cook in soups and other dishes.

NUTS

Almonds are the king of nuts and the only alkaline nut. Other nuts that are nutritious, although acid forming, are pecans, filberts, walnuts, brazil nuts and pinon.

SEEDS

Sunflower, pumpkin, sesame, flax, chia, psyllium.

VEGETABLES

Potatoes (red, sweet, and yams have more protein and Vitamin C than Irish potatoes, white), carrots, cauliflower, artichokes, asparagus, squash (yellow, zucchini, acorn, hubbard, spaghetti), green beans, tomatoes, beets and beet greens, broccoli, brussel sprouts, red and green cabbage, Chinese cabbage, celery, collards, corn, cucumber, endive, kale, Jerusalem artichokes, mushrooms, leeks, onions, lettuce (Romaine, bibb, red leaf), kohlribi, okra, parsley, green peppers, parsnips, peas, pumpkins, turnips, watercress (to name a few).

FRUITS

Apples (all varieties), pears, apricots, peaches, avocados, bananas, blackberries, raspberries, blueberries, strawberries, cherries, cantaloupe, casaba melon, watermelon, cranberries, oranges, honeydew melon, mangos, papayas, persimmons, pineapple, plums, pomegranate, prunes, tangerine and rhubbard.

HERBS AND SPICES

Garlic, ginger root, onions, parsley, basil, sage, tumeric, curry, bay leaft, cardamon, chili powder, coriader, cumin, dill, fennel, marjoram, mustard seed, oregano, paprika, cayenne, cinnamon, nutmeg, rosemary, saffron, tarragon.

FISH

Bass, cod, flounder, haddock, halibut, perch, pike, sole, salmon, red snapper, trout. Any other **scaled** fresh water or ocean fish is acceptable.

MEAT

Beef, lamb, chicken and turkey (should be free of hormones, chemicals and antibiotics). Call a health food store for information on where to find these particular products. Whole grain casseroles are a good meat dish replacement.

SEA VEGETABLES

Agar-agar, dulse, kelp, kombu, and nori.

THE HOW, WHERE, AND WHEN OF SEXY EATING

FOOD PREPARATION

Every cell in the body eats, digests and eliminates waste products just as we do. The wonderful life in food is the same life we have within us. What would happen to your life if I threw you in boiling oil, boiling water, or in a 450 degree oven, just as many of us do with our food? Your body chemistry would undergo a deadly change. On the other hand, if I placed you in a sauna or steam bath for a few minutes, would you survive? Of course! **Steaming, cooking or baking foods at low heat maintains nutritional value.**

GRAZING FOR SEXUAL VITALITY

It has been said that **"Life is more digestible if it is sipped, not gulped."**

Many of us tend to be gluttons at meal time. This unhealthy habit may be attributed to the typical American habit of waiting three to five hours or longer between meals. Such a time span between meals depletes the blood sugar, leaving us feeling tired and famished. By the time we do eat, our blood sugar may be so low that we tend to over eat and yet never feel full. Gluttony is a harmful practice, since the "stuffing" of food only serves to overwork the digestive system. Food is digested and absorbed very poorly when such eating habits are followed, tending to encourage fat storage and poor assimilation of nutrients.

"Grazing" is a term which best describes the eating patterns of healthy cultures. **Eating several small meals a day is the healthiest practice to follow.** Several small snacks a day (four to six) stabilizes the blood sugar level without over-working or overfilling the stomach and other digestive organs. In its healthy and mature state, your stomach is about the size of your fist. It only needs a small amount of food to be filled and thereby satisfied. This can best be accomplished by frequent, small meals.

Have you ever noticed the way small children eat? They are satisfied with several small meals a day. They may eat half a banana, run outside to play, come back in an hour for a little cheese, then run back outside again. Children prefer snacking throughout the day to eating three large meals. However, parents are taught that eating between meals spoils a child's appetite. Therefore, they starve their children for several hours and then expect them to eat a large meal like "grown-ups." **The three meal a day habit makes gluttons out of children who are natural "grazers."**

Many of my clients ask me if eating so many small meals overworks the digestive organs. The answer is no, but too much food at one meal certainly does. Does breathing over and over again hurt the lungs? If it did, a person would have to take one gigantic breath and hold it in for three hours! It is natural to put food in the digestive tract. **Frequent, small meals will discourage over-eating and gluttony.**

BREAKFAST

Breakfast is considered by many nutrition experts to be the most important meal of the day. This meal should consist of grains (see recipes), in order to keep our blood sugar stable until noon. Feeling full for a few hours after eating a grain meal is a sign that your blood sugar is stable. **"Eat like a king at breakfast, like a queen at lunch, and like a pauper at dinner,"** was an adage of a popular nutritionist. Many Americans eat little or no breakfast and indulge in a huge meal at dinner. If you eat a large and late dinner, you probably will not be hungry in the morning. And if you are one of those people who does not feel hungry in the morning, follow this simple rule: Never eat more at dinner than you ate at breakfast. If you didn't eat breakfast, don't eat dinner. I can guarantee that you will be hungry the next morning.

LUNCH

This meal often must vary according to circumstance and convenience. Many fast food chains have salad bars, an excellent choice for lunch. Seek out natural food restaurants or cafeterias near your place of employment or bring your own lunch to work (see recipes).

DINNER

I suggest that dinner be a family meal at home if possible. In the United States today, 50% of all food dollars are spent **outside the home** at fast-food chains. This unhealthy practice is expensive and contributes to poor nutrition as well as the breakdown of marriages and families. **Bring your family together at dinner!**

Grains should be included in this meal if not eaten at lunch. **For increased general energy as well as sexual energy, improved elimination, grains should be eaten at breakfast and again at lunch or dinner.**

129

SNACKS

If energy is low, eat protein snacks such as almonds, sunflower seeds or yogurt. Fruits also are delicious snacks, but can upset blood sugar levels unless eaten with protein. A few almonds eaten with fruit will stabilize the blood sugar. **Do not wait longer than two hours between snacks.** Very light snacks may also be eaten in the evening if necessary, however, restful sleep is assured if protein is not eaten too late at night, since protein takes at least eight hours to digest. **Make sure your stomach is asleep before you are.**

TIPS FOR GETTING THE MOST OUT OF WHAT YOU EAT

1. Eat in a calm and peaceful setting. **It is better not to eat when you are angry, nervous or otherwise upset.**

2. **Chew your food well** (20-40 times is optimum). If you must eat in a hurry, eat a very small meal. By eating slowly you allow your digestive system to catch up with your mouth. Many people who have lived over 100 years practice this fundamental rule.

3. **Stop eating when you are full.** If you practice the "three-meals-and-five-snacks-a-day-plan," you will feel fuller sooner.

4. **Eating should be based on enjoyment, not denial.** No one likes a reducing diet, because starvation is no fun. Denial is not the way to health anymore than is overeating.

5. **Eat natural foods whenever possible.** Other than whole grains, bewans, nuts and seeds which are protected by an outer covering, wholesome, fresh, live food is very fragile and spoils if left unrefrigerated overnight. **Eat foods which can spoil, decay and rot.** Most canned, frozen or otherwise processed foods contain additives for color, taste, and preser-

vation, making them potentially hazardous to our health. Read labels carefully and avoid chemical additives. Support your local health food stores and encourage the manager of your local grocery to develop a health food section within the store. Shopping at natural food stores will increase your knowledge of health and enable you to meet new friends. **The road to health has many nice people on it!**

6. **Drink before or after meals. Drinking liquids with main meals dilutes your digestive juices and inhibits food digestion.** Drink 30 minutes before or 30 minutes after a meal. Drinking with snacks will cause no digestive problems.

7. **The best digestive aid is exercise.** Although daily exercise is essential to good digestion, do not eat immediately before or after intense physical or mental exertion. Read the chapter on exercise for further guidelines.

TIPS FOR REPLACING UNSEXY FOODS

"The easiest way to eliminate a bad habit is to develop a healthier one in its place." Nature abhors a vacuum. Whenever a vacuum is created, something will always fill it. Saying "no" to foods such as sugar, salt, fats, and processed food will not accomplish the final goal of better health. "No" is not enough; "yes" is also required. Many people say to me, "I don't eat sugar, why am I having blood sugar problems?" Eliminating refined sugar only begins to solve the hypoglycemic problem. A person must also eat complex carbohydrates which provide the body with the necessary natural sugar. The replacement/substitution strategy will make the dietary transition easier as well as more healthy.

SWEETIN' UP YOUR LOVE LIFE

SWEETENERS

If grains and fruits are not enough to satisfy your "sweet tooth" at the beginning of your new diet, use barley, malt syrup, or fruit juices such as pineapple, grape and apple for sweeteners. Barley malt and apple juice concentrate syrups can be added to bakery goods and plain yogurt.

SPICE UP YOUR LOVE LIFE

CONDIMENTS

Black pepper, which is very irritating to the stomach lining, should be replaced with cayenne (red pepper). There are a number of products in your health food store which will provide a "salty" taste. Remember that tamari or soya sauce are very high in salt content. Don't forget to experiment with herbs and spices when cooking (see list of herbs and spices in chapter 1) to find ways of pleasantly enhancing your foods without the addition of salt and black pepper. Most health food and grocery stores carry fresh herbs and information books to guide you to their use.

DRESS UP YOUR LOVE LIFE

SALAD DRESSING

Natural salad dressings contain some honey and a little sea salt are acceptable alternatives to regular commercial dressings. Olive oil and lemon are a wonderful addition to any salad. Create your own salad dressings in a blender using foods such as yogurt, avocado, lemon, herbs, apple cider vinegar, and vegetable broth powder. When dining out, ask for vinegar and oil dressing which contains no salt or sugar.

BUTTER UP YOUR LOVE LIFE

UNSALTED BUTTER

Margarine is a processed food which is partially hydrogenated. In the processing of polyunsaturated oils, hydrogen is forced back into the molecular structure of fatty acids which makes the oil "solid" at room temperature. Our bodies have great difficulty breaking down hydrogenated oil, which can lead to arterial problems. Unsalted butter can be found in health food stores or the "butter section" of most supermarkets. It may safely be used in moderation (one or two pats a day).

NUT BUTTERS

Nut butters such as almond or sesame (tahini) are excellent substitutes for peanut butter. They taste very good on unsalted rye crisps or rice cakes. Raw, unsalted nut butter is best.

COFFEE SUBSTITUTES

Cafix, Pero, Postum and other cereal coffee replace coffee while herb teas replace commercial black teas which contain tannic acid and caffeine. Herbs are medicine and best taken for specific conditions. Peppermint and Camomile are exceptions.

ALCOHOLIC BEVERAGES

If you must drink alcohol, dry white wine contains the least amount of sugar, of all the varities of wine. Natural, light beers are best of the beers. Fresh fruit and vegetable juices are great substitute for alcoholic beverages. **These juices give you a natural high with no hangover.**

LUNCH MEATS

Avocado or guacomole, fish, natural chicken or turkey and nut butters are fine substitutes for highly processed luncheon meats which are high in fat, nitrates, and nitrites (possibly cancer producing).

SOUPS

Instead of canned or packaged soups high in salt, preservatives and chemicals, create your own homemade soups in a crock pot. Crock pots use low heat and don't require constant attention. Putting a cup or more of grains like brown rice, barley or millet into any soup makes a "hardier," thicker, delicious and more filling meal. Use rice flour rather than wheat to thicken soups. Natural food cookbooks contain numerous recipes (see list in back of this book).

BREAD

Eat 100% cooked, whole grains (millet, brown rice, buckwheat, barley, oats, etc.) in place of bread. Many people crave starch because it converts to sugar or glucose when digested. Whole grains satisfy starch cravings and provide slowly digesting sugar as well. If you must eat bread products, 100% sourdough rye bread, flourless sprouted bread, unsalted rye crisps, rice cakes and corn tortillias are the best choices. Use rice flour, oat flour, soy flour or buckwheat flour as substitutes when bread recipes call for wheat flour.

CANNED FOODS

Fresh vegetables and fruits are preferable to frozen. In turn, frozen foods are preferable to canned foods. You waste your hard-earned money on canned foods; canned food is dead food! How much life would you have left after spending time in a sealed can?

SUBSTITUTE HERBS FOR DRUGS

Common over-the-counter drugs such as aspirin, antacids, laxatives, cold remedies and cough syrups deplete the sex glands and should be replaced with natural herbs in capsules, extracts, essences and tinctures. These herbs can be found at local health food stores. **Substitute herbs for drugs whenever possible.** Your local health food store carries books on herbs which will provide advice regarding proper usage for common ailments. **Caution:** Herbal combinations are medicine and should be taken for specific problems and for specific lengths of time. You wouldn't continually take an aspirin to prevent a possible headache, and you shouldn't take herbal formulas, designed for special ailments, all the time.

BOTTLED WATER

Growing evidence reveals that chemicals added to purify public water systems are dangerous and even cancer producing (see unsexy foods for explanation). Since water is essential to good health, consider drinking bottled water.

Spring water, low in sodium content, is the preferred bottled water. This water is sold in supermarkets and health food stores and distributed by private water companies. I recommend drinking distilled water for a cleansing period of three to six months only. If you wish to continue drinking distilled water after this initial cleansing period, add two tablespoons of sea water per gallon for remineralization. Your local health food store should carry sea water or know where it may be purchased. An economical way to obtain distilled water is to make your own! Many companies manufacture home distillers.

BINGE — I CAN

"What many of us need most is a vigorous kick in the seat of our can'ts!"

135

When beginning a new diet, we have great expectations and inspiration. But there comes that day when we inevitably "go off" our diet and junk out. In a moment of weakness we will eat some junk foods we may have been dreaming about for weeks. Our self-esteem slips during such binges and we beat ourselves up by saying, "Oh, well, I blew it; it's all over. I'm a bad person. I just can't do anything right."

My suggestion to you is to deliberately include a binge in your eating program. If your diet includes a chance to kick up your heels once in a while and eat things you don't normally eat, it will be easier to "stay on your diet." Generally "diets" are considered to be a form of punishment because we stop eating the foods we enjoy. Actually, the word diet is derived from the Greek word, diaita, meaning "a manner of living" or way of life. The wise person is not interested in changing his diet, but rather changing his lifestyle, to improve his health and sex life. Life is not something you can go on and off of. **Developing a healthy lifestyle for sexual vitality requires consistency but not absolute perfection.** Take a look at society's idea of success. It is much less than perfect. For instance, a successful batter has a batting average of .300. According to this average, the batter fails two out of every three times he comes to the plate. Another sport example involves football. A quarterback who is considered successful completes at least 50% of his passes. Although one out of every two passes are not complete, the quarterback is looked upon as very successful. If you can improve your lifestyle by 50%, your performance is probably 100% better than before.

Thomas Edison failed in 1000 consecutive experiments before he finally invented the light bulb. When asked, "How could you continue after so many failures?" he replied, "I don't consider those failures, I think of them as 1000 ways how not to make a light bulb." This is a successful attitude. Every experiment ending in failure provided Edison with another piece of the puzzle, ultimately leading to a successful invention. While developing your healthy lifestyle, begin to think, **"I will make all my failures and mistakes part of my ultimate success."** These failures are part of the process leading you to ultimate victory.

In the 1982 New York marathon, one inspiring story was told about a woman who ran the race on crutches. It took her more than eleven hours to complete the race, she fell eleven times, and **completed** the race in the dark of the night after everyone else had gone home. The importance of this story is that although she fell eleven times, she got up eleven times, finishing the marathon.

Dr. Paavo Airola discovered that the people in all the healthy cultures he studied occasionally binged! He found that these cultures celebrated a festival or a religious holiday approximately thirty days, during which time they ate and drank in excess. After the day of partying was over, the people returned to their wholesome diets.

CONCLUSION

The OH! YES! diet is a lifestyle change which will help bring life back into your tired sex glands and return you to the youthful state that you were meant to experience. It is a return to the diet the human body has adapted to over thousands of years, and it emphasizes whole, fresh foods. These foods are sexy foods because they are foods that came from seeds, the most potent, powerful, and fertile sources of vitamins, minerals, proteins, carbohydrates, fats, and enzymes in this planet.

The OH! YES! diet has a proven track record. The cultures mentioned earlier have lived on this diet for generations and with complete success. There is no more convincing evidence than learning from people who have lived a hundred years or more! Following is an excerpt page from Dr. Paavo Airola's book, *Rejuvenation Secrets From Around the World*, Health Plus Publishers. These centenarians quoted are both from Russia.

"One man, **126** years old told me:
I've worked hard all of my life, but never had much money to worry about. I walk at least 5 miles

every day, and ride a horse. I eat very little, and only when hungry—I never eat at regular times, but just when I feel really hungry. **I was married four times, each time to a younger wife. Maybe this has helped me to stay young!**

The Russian Minister of Health told a story of a Russian centenarian from Caucasus who lived to the respectable age of **146** years. When asked for the reasons for his eviable longevity the man said:

I've never had a boss over me. I have never been envious of what others have. **And I have periodically rejuvenated myself by marrying three times!**

The above two cases seem to demonstrate that vibrant health, long life, and sexual virility go hand in hand. Dr. Bernard Jensen, who has studied the lives of centenarians in Russia, Turkey, and Bulgaria, made a similar observation. Upon his return, he said:

"I've made a remarkable observation: almost all centenarians I've met have been married several times.

My conclusion is that we do not stop sexual activity because we grow old—we grow old because we stop sexual activity."

The OH! YES! diet will work for you. Start today applying the principles contained in it, and you will enjoy a better sex life tonight.

6

Eat and Enjoy! OH! YES! Diet! Recipes For Lovers

"Nothin says lovin, like somethin from the oven."

Substituting good quality, low fat protein entrees from grain, fish and chicken sources will help build and maintain Optimum Health for Youth, Energy and Sex (OH! YES!). Including plenty of garlic, olive oil, seeds, almonds, vegetables and fruits in your daily OH! YES! diet will insure a healthy interest and "staying power" throughout your sex life.

Any recipe can be "cleaned up," including the ones to follow, by substituting **Vegit** or **Dr. Jensen's Vegetable Broth Powder** for salt or sea salt. A little unrefined, raw honey occasionally will not harm you. Other alternatives for refined sugar are **Dr. Jensen's Apple Juice Concentrate** (a syrup) and **barley malt syrup.** An excellent substitute for soy sauce or tamari sauce (high in salt) is **Dr. Jensen's Quick Sip.** All can be purchased at a health food store or write to:

> Bernard Jensen Products
> Route 1, Box 52
> Escondido, CA 92025

Other fine recipes are included in the cook books list in the back of the book. **Remember whole grains are vital foods to energize your sex life.**

139

BREAKFAST SUGGESTIONS

OUTSTANDING OATS
(my clients' favorite breakfast)

Soak ½ cup rolled oats and 2 tbsp. currants in distilled water
overnight.

In the morning:
Pour off water from oats and add:

1 banana (sliced)
1 tbsp. plain yogurt (optional)
1 grated apple (optional)
10 almonds (grind in blender) or whole
Stir and enjoy.

For hot oatmeal:

Pour boiling water over ½ cup rolled oats and currants,
cover and steep for 5 minutes. Pour off water and add
above ingredients. (*LPG)

SOURDOUGH RYE BREAD

8 cups freshly-ground whole rye flour
3 cups warm water
½ cup sourdough culture

Mix 7 cups of flour with the water and sourdough culture.
Cover and let stand in a warm place for 12 to 18 hours.
Add remaining flour, mix well, and knead for 5 minutes,
using a dough mixer if you have one. Place in buttered
and floured pans. Let rise in a warm place for approximately 1-2 hours or until the loaf has risen noticeably.
Always save ½ cup of dough as a culture for the next
baking, it will be necessary to obtain a sourdough culture from a friend or from a commercial baker.

Preheat oven to 350-400° F. and bake for 1 hour or more, if needed. This recipe makes one 2-pound loaf.

Sourdough bread baking is a delicate art. If you do not succeed at first, don't give up—keep experimenting until you bake a sublimely delicious loaf that will not only fill your house with Old-Country aroma, but will delight your family and justify the Biblical reference to bread as the "Staff of Life." (*CAD)

WAERLAND FIVE-GRAIN KRUSKA

1 tablespoon whole wheat
1 tablespoon whole rye
1 tablespoon whole barley
1 tablespoon whole millet
1 tablespoon whole oats
1 tablespoon wheat bran
2 tablespoons unsulfured raisins
1-1½ cups water

Grind the 5 grains coarsely in your grinder. Place all ingredients in a pot and boil for 5-10 minutes, then wrap the pot in a blanket or newspapers and let it stand for a few hours. Experiment with the amount of water used. Kruska must not be mushy but should have the consistency of a very thick porridge. Serve hot with sweet milk and Homemade Applesauce or stewed fruits. Makes 4 servings.

This is another cereal that can be used by those who have a tendency towards constipation. (*CAD)

BUCKWHEAT PANCAKES

1 cup whole raw buckwheat or buckwheat flour
½ cup rolled oats
2 eggs
2 cups buttermilk, yogurt, or kefir

Place buckwheat and oats or fresh wheat germ in blender or
seed grinder and grind well until a fine flour is obtained.
Mix flour in a medium-sized bowl with remaining ingredients and blend well. If batter is too thick, add fresh
milk to desired consistency. Fry on a lightly-buttered
griddle on low heat.

Serve with butter, olive oil, or Homemade Applesauce.
Makes 6 delicious medium-sized pancakes. (*CAD)

FRESH FRUIT SALAD WITH YOGURT DRESSING

2 cups pineapple cut into 1 inch cubes
2 cups fresh strawberries
1 cup sliced fresh peaches
2 tablespoons ground almonds
2 medium bananas, sliced
1 cup fresh green grapes
1 cup plain yogurt
2 tablespoons orange juice

Combine the fruits in a large bowl. Mix the yogurt and orange
juice and pour over the fruit salad. Sprinkle almonds
over fruit and yogurt. (*CAD)

GRAIN ENTREES FOR SEXUAL ENERGY

LENTIL BARLEY STEW

1 cup lentils
⅓ cup barley
3 cups water
2 cups Homemade Stewed Tomatoes
¼ cup chopped onion
¼ cup chopped celery
¼ cup chopped carrots
1 clove garlic, minced
sea salt to taste
dash of cayenne pepper

Cook the lentils and barley together in the 3 cups of water until tender, about 1½ hours. Add the stewed tomatoes, onion, celery, carrots, garlic, sea salt and cayenne and mix together. Pour into a casserole dish and bake at 350° F. for 35-40 minutes. (*CAD)

MILLET WITH ONIONS

2 cups cooked millet
1 onion, sliced
1 clove garlic, minced
2 tablespoons sesame
1 tablespoon chopped parsley
½ teaspoon sea salt

Saute the sliced onions and garlic in 2 tablespoons water just until tender, about 5 minutes. Add more water if needed. Stir in the cooked millet, oil, parsley and sea salt. Cook over medium heat a few minutes to heat through. Serves 4.

MILLET AND TOMATOES

2 cups cooked millet
½ cup chopped celery
⅓ cup chopped onion
1 clove of garlic, minced
1 cup chopped fresh tomatoes
2 tablespoons olive oil
½ teaspoon sea salt
sour cream or yogurt

Water saute the celery, onion and garlic in 2 tablespoons water 5 minutes. Add more water if necessary. Stir in the chopped tomatoes, olive oil, sea salt and cooked millet. Cook 5 minutes to heat through. Serve with a spoonful of yogurt or sour cream on top. Makes 4 servings. (*CAD)

WOK VEGGIES AND RICE

3 cups water
1 cup brown rice

Boil water, add rice (millet may be substituted), simmer for 45 minutes, or bake in oven at 350° with 2 cups water, 1 cup brown rice. Fifteen minutes before rice is done, cook veggies in wok or saute in pan. (Use sesame oil or olive oil and Quick Sip.)

1 large carrot
½ leek or onion
2 small red potatoes
⅓ lb. of firm tofu or chicken (optional)
1 cup kale, broccoli or cauliflower

Add cooked rice and continue stirring 2 minutes over medium heat. (*LPG)

STUFFED GREEN PEPPER

4 green bell peppers
1 cup chopped fresh mushrooms
½ cup chopped onions
½ cup chopped celery
1 clove of garlic, minced
½ cup Homemade Tomato Sauce
1 tablespoon chopped parsley
2 cups cooked brown rice
2 tablespoons olive oil

Wash the green peppers. Remove the seeds and membranes. Water saute the chopped mushrooms, onion,
celery and garlic in ¼ cup water until tender, about 5
minutes. Add more water if necessary. Stir in the olive
oil, tomato sauce, parsley and cooked brown rice. Stuff
the green peppers with the mixture. Place in a baking
dish. Bake at 350° for 20-30 minutes or until the green
peppers are tender. Serves 4. (*CAD)

BLACK BEANS AND RICE

1½ cups dried black beans
1 cup chopped onion
1 clove of garlic, minced
1 teaspoon sea salt
cooked brown rice

Cover the beans with water in a large saucepan and soak
overnight. Add the onions and garlic and simmer 2½
hours or until tender. Add more water if needed. When
cooked, add the sea salt. Serve over brown rice. Makes 6
servings. (*CAD)

SWEDISH CABBAGE ROLLS

1 large head cabbage
3 cups cooked brown rice
2 eggs, slightly beaten
¼ cup chopped onions
¼ cup chopped celery
¼ cup chopped green pepper
2 cups Homemade Tomato Sauce
1 clove of garlic, minced
½ teaspoon ground allspice
½ teaspoon sea salt
dash of cayenne pepper

Cut the core out of the cabbage and place the cabbage in a large pot of boiling water. Pull off the outer leaves as soon as they become tender. You will need 8-10 leaves. Let them cool.

Mix together the cooked brown rice, eggs, onion, celery, green pepper, 1 cup of the tomato sauce, garlic, allspice, sea salt and cayenne.

Place a large spoonful of filling on each cabbage leaf. Then, fold the right and left sides of the leaf over the filling. Roll up, starting at the bottom of the leaf. The cabbage roll may be held together with a wooden toothpick, tied with thread or placed seam side down in the baking dish. Pour the remaining 1 cup of tomato sauce over the cabbage rolls. Bake in a covered casserole dish at 350° for 30-40 minutes. Makes 4-5 servings. (*CAD)

FISH AND CHICKEN ENTREES FOR
SEXUAL ENERGY

HERB-BROILED SALMON STEAKS

½ cup melted butter
2 teaspoons seasoned salt
½ teaspoon garlic powder
½ teaspoon lemon peel
2 lbs. salmon steaks
2 teaspoons lemon juice
1 teaspoon tarragon
½ teaspoon ground marjoram
dash cayenne or red pepper

Combine melted butter and lemon juice with seasonings. Arrange salmon steaks on greased broiler rack and brush with one-half of seasoned butter. Broil 2 inches from heat 5 to 10 minutes. Carefully turn and brush with remaining butter mixture. Broil steaks 7 minutes longer or until they can be flaked easily with a fork. Serve hot, garnished with lemon wedges and sprigs of parsley. (*CGF)

MOUTH-WATERING BAKED FISH

8 to 10 lb. fish
   (salmon, sea bass, red snapper, etc.)
½ cup onion flakes
¼ cup lemon juice
4 cloves fresh garlic, minced or pressed
Salt and pepper to taste
Paprika
non-stick vegetable spray
¼ cup brandy or apple juice
¼ cup oil or melted butter
¼ cup soya sauce
2 tablespoons Worcestershire sauce
Lemon slices

Rinse and dry fish and put into baking dish that has been sprayed with a vegetable non-stick spray. Combine all ingredients and pour over fish. Let stand at least one hour. Bake in 400° oven for about 30 minutes or until fish flakes and has lost its transparency. Baste at least once during baking process. Decorate top with lemon slices and paprika. (*CGF)

BASS AND SWISS CHARD

2 tablespoons olive oil
salt and pepper to taste
4 cloves fresh garlic, minced
2 cans (1 lb. each) solid pack tomatoes
1 whole bass, about 4 lbs.
2 large bunches Swiss chard
2 medium onions, chopped

In large covered roasting pan or casserole, place oil and then bass; sprinkle with salt and pepper. Cut chard in 3-inch pieces and lay on top of bass with garlic and onion. Pour tomatoes on top. Bake at 350° for 1½ hours with cover on. Remove cover and bake another ½ hour. Serve immediately from the baking dish. (*CGF)

GIN-GAR CHICKEN

8 oz. plain yogurt
1 1-inch square piece ginger root
1½ tsp. salt
8 cloves fresh garlic
1½ tsp. chili powder
1-2 ½ lb. broiler-fryer chicken cut up
    (or equivalent parts)

Put a small amount of yogurt in blender; add garlic and ginger and puree until smooth. Remove from blender and stir into remaining yogurt; add spices and blend well. Pour over chicken and marinate in covered container overnight, 12 to 24 hours, shaking occasionally. Cook over hot coals. Serve hot or cold with lemon slices. (*CGF)

FORTY-CLOVE CHICKEN FILICE

1 frying chicken, cut in pieces
½ cup dry white wine
¼ cup olive oil
1 tsp. oregano
2 tsp. dry basil
pinch of crushed red pepper
40 cloves fresh garlic
¼ cup dry vermouth
4 stalks celery, cut in 1-inch pieces
6 sprigs minced parsley

Place chicken pieces into shallow baking pan, skin side up. Sprinkle all ingredients evenly over top of chicken. Squeeze juice from lemon and pour over top. Cut remaining lemon rind into pieces and arrange throughout chicken. Cover with foil and bake at 375° for 40 minutes. Remove foil and bake an additional 15 minutes. (*CGF)

SOUP UP YOUR SEX LIFE

LENTIL SOUP

1 cup lentils
1 stalk celery, chopped
1 medium carrot, chopped
⅓ cup chopped onion
1 clove of garlic, minced
3 cups water

¼ cup lemon juice
¼ teaspoon sea salt
¼ teaspoon granular kelp

Simmer the lentils, celery, carrots, onion, and garlic in water
1½ hours, until tender. Add the lemon juice, sea salt,
and kelp and cook another 5 minutes. Serves 4-6. (*CAD)

BEAN SOUP

2 cups dry pinto beans
6 cups water
2 medium carrots, diced
1 onion, chopped
1 stalk celery with tops, chopped
1 teaspoon chili powder
sea salt to taste

Soak the beans overnight in the water and then cook until
tender, 3-4 hours. Add the diced carrots, chopped
onions, and celery. Simmer until the vegetables are
tender, about one hour. Add the chili powder and sea
salt about ½ hour before the beans are finished. Makes
4-6 servings. (*CAD)

SPLIT PEA SOUP

1 cup dried split peas
3 cups water
½ cup chopped onion
1 small carrot, diced
1 stalk celery, diced
1 teaspoon sea salt

Wash peas, place in a saucepan with the vegetables, and
cover with water. Bring to a boil. Reduce heat and

simmer for 1½ hours or until peas are tender. Add sea salt and your favorite herb seasonings. Puree in the blender or serve as is. Makes 4-6 servings. (*CAD)

MAMA'S POTATO SOUP

2 tbsp. oil
1 cup finely chopped onion
3 medium-sized tomatoes, peeled and chopped
1 tbsp. flour
2½ cups peeled raw potatoes, cut into small cubes
2 medium-sized carrots, peeled and thinly sliced
2 cups Monterey Jack cheese, cut into small cubes
4 cloves fresh garlic, minced
½ cup chopped green chiles
2 quarts hot chicken broth
2 tsp. salt (or to taste)
1 tsp. black pepper
1 medium-sized zucchini, thinly sliced

Heat oil in 3-quart saucepan and add garlic, onions, tomatoes and green chiles; saute for 3 minutes. Stir in flour and cook for 2 more minutes. Continue stirring as you pour in the hot broth. Add potatoes, salt and pepper. Cover pan and simmer over low heat for 20 minutes. Add carrots and zucchini and cook for 15 minutes longer or until potatoes are tender. Just before serving add the cubed cheese. Makes 4 to 6 servings. (*CGF)

AVOCADO BISQUE

2 bunches spinach, heated until just wilted but not cooked
4 to 5 cloves fresh garlic
1 cup chicken broth
1 tsp. salt
2 medium-sized California avocados

1 cup half-and-half
1 tbsp. butter

Place all ingredients in blender and blend 45 seconds until creamy smooth. Pour into a saucepan and cover. Heat on medium until puffs of steam are seen at top. Do not allow to boil, as avocados will become bitter. Serve immediately. Makes about 1 quart.

SWEETEN UP YOUR SEX LIFE

HALVAH

1 cup hulled sesame seeds
2 teaspoons honey, preferably pollen rich, unfiltered

Grind sesame seeds in a small electric seed grinder. Pour sesame meal into a small bowl and knead honey into the meal with a large spoon until honey is well mixed in and the halvah acquires the consistency of a hard dough. Serve it as is or make small balls and roll them in whole sesame seeds or sunflower seeds. This is an excellent, nutritious, and delicious candy, loved by children and grown-ups alike. (*CAD)

TROPICAL YOGURT DELIGHT

½ banana
3 tablespoons fresh papaya
2 tablespoons yogurt
few drops lemon or lime juice

Mash all ingredients together with a fork or potato masher. (*CAD)

JUICE POPSICLES

Pour fresh juice (apple, orange, grape, watermelon, etc.) into
ice cube trays or popsicle holders and freeze.

BANANA LOGS

Ripe bananas
Plain yogurt
Sesame seeds, freshly grated coconut, or chopped
    sunflower seeds

Peel the bananas and cut into 1-inch pieces. Dip each piece
    into the yogurt and then roll in the sesame seeds,
    grated coconut or chopped sunflower seeds. (*CAD)

OATMEAL RAISIN COOKIES

½ cup raisins
½ cup hot water
½ cup butter
¾ cup honey
1 teaspoon natural vanilla extract
2 cups whole wheat flour or brown rice
1 teaspoon baking soda
1 teaspoon ground cinnamon
2 cups rolled oats

Soak the raisins in the hot water 20-30 minutes. Cream the
    butter and honey together. Add the eggs, vanilla, and
    the water the raisins were soaking in. Sift the dry ingre-
    dients together and add to the liquid ingredients. Add
    the raisins and rolled oats. Drop by spoonfuls 2 inches
    apart on a buttered baking sheet. Bake at 400 degrees,
    8-10 minutes. (*CAD)

ALMOND TREATS

½ cup pecans
½ cup walnuts
1½ teaspoons cinnamon
½ teaspoon sea salt (optional)
¼ to ½ almond butter
½ cup almonds, blanched
¼ cup currants
½ teaspoon cardamom
2 or 3 tablespoons organic maple syrup

Mix all ingredients together and roll into balls. Either walnuts or pecans can be omitted but not both. May use whole or chopped nuts. Makes 12 balls.

ALMOND NUT PIE

1½ cups almonds
1⅓ cups barley malt syrup
4 eggs beaten
freshly ground nutmeg (to taste)
2 tbsp. melted butter (unsalted)
1 teaspoon vanilla

Combine ingredients, pour in pie shell and bake at 350° for about 25 minutes.

OATMEAL PIE CRUST

1½ cups oat flakes
¼ cup sesame oil
¾ cup brown rice flour
½ cup cold water (bottled)

Dry roast oat flakes until lightly browned, mix with flour, add oil and mix very well with fork. Then add water slowly,

154

mix well. Let sit for 15-30 minutes, then press into pie pan. Bake 10 minutes at 350° before filling or bake 30 minutes for unfilled pie shell.

CUDDLEY CAROB CANDY
(for chocolate lovers)

½ cup raw sunflower seeds
½ cup currants
¼ cup almond milk
½ cup sliced almonds
2 tbsp. almond butter

Melt 1 cup unsweetened carob chips in double boiler, add 2 tbsp. sesame butter or almond butter, then add other ingredients. (*LPG)

*CGF — Courtesy of Gilroy Garlic Festival
*CAD — Courtesy of The Airola Diet and Cookbook
*LPG — Courtesy of The Lazy Person's Guide To Better Nutrition

Love Stewy

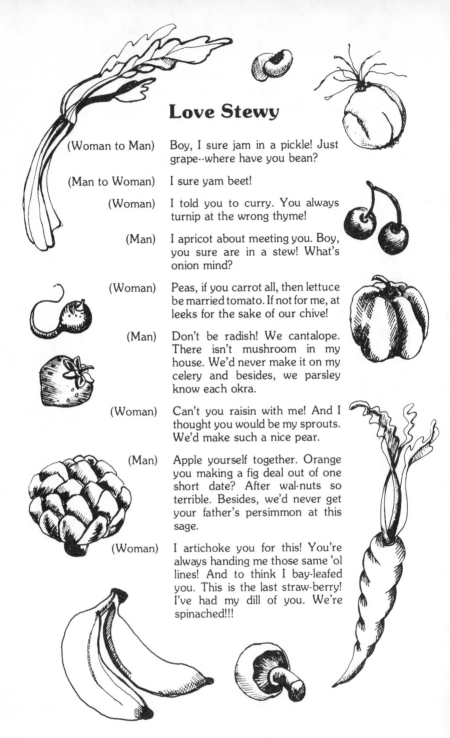

(Woman to Man) Boy, I sure jam in a pickle! Just grape--where have you bean?

(Man to Woman) I sure yam beet!

(Woman) I told you to curry. You always turnip at the wrong thyme!

(Man) I apricot about meeting you. Boy, you sure are in a stew! What's onion mind?

(Woman) Peas, if you carrot all, then lettuce be married tomato. If not for me, at leeks for the sake of our chive!

(Man) Don't be radish! We cantalope. There isn't mushroom in my house. We'd never make it on my celery and besides, we parsley know each okra.

(Woman) Can't you raisin with me! And I thought you would be my sprouts. We'd make such a nice pear.

(Man) Apple yourself together. Orange you making a fig deal out of one short date? After wal-nuts so terrible. Besides, we'd never get your father's persimmon at this sage.

(Woman) I artichoke you for this! You're always handing me those same 'ol lines! And to think I bay-leafed you. This is the last straw-berry! I've had my dill of you. We're spinached!!!

7

"Aphrodisiacs" and Natural Hormones: Love At First Bite

"Sexual energy is sparked by excess energy."

—Dr. Paavo Airola

An aphrodisiac is defined as a food or medicine which increases or excites sexual desire. I do not advocate or recommend any artificial stimulation for those with a normal, healthy, sex drive. **Optimum health is the best aphrodisiac.** However, when sexual activity or interest is disturbed or reduced due to physical weakness, poor health, hormonal inadequacies, and glandular disorders, improved nutrition and special virility foods are in order to help improve sexual activity.

While we won't even discuss potentially harmful drugs or worthless magic potions, **there are foods and food substance used and recommended as aphrodisiacs by many cultures.** In all cultural traditions we find references to "amorous foods" that stir sexual passion and maintain sexual activity. The Chinese, Japanese, Arabs, Hindus and Europeans, as well as many ancient civilizations have faithfully used these food stimulants and rejuvenators for hundreds of years with apparent success. These foods do not cause artificial stimulation of sex centers or glands. They feed nutritionally-starved endocrine glands and stimulate sex hormone production. There is no promise of **"love at first bite,"** but in

157

conjunction with the OH! YES! diet **these additional supports should, given time, help to correct subnormal sexual desires and sexual activity by contributing to the overall health of the endocrine glands and increasing the sex hormone production.**

ALMONDS

Although all nuts are excellent for building and maintaining sexual energy, almonds are often called, **"The King of Nuts."** They contain generous amounts of calcium, magnesium, potassium, iron, B vitamins, Vitamin E, and protein, all nutrients vital for healthy sex glands.

COMPARISON: ALMOND vs. MILK (3½ oz.)				
NUTRIENT	ALMOND Raw Unsalted	*COW'S MILK 3.5% fat	COW'S MILK 3.7% fat	*SKIM MILK
CALCIUM	234mg	118mg	117mg	121mg
PROTEIN	18.6mg	3.5mg	3.5mg	3.6mg
FIBER	2.6mg	0	0	0
PHOSPHORUS	504mg	93mg	92mg	95mg
IRON	4.7mg	trace	trace	trace
POTASSIUM	773mg	144mg	140mg	145mg
THIAMINE	.24mg	.03mg	.03mg	.04mg
RIBOFLAVIN	.92mg	.17mg	.17mg	.18mg

*Pasteurized and raw

Source: U.S. Department of Agriculture Handbook #8.

According to the Bible, almonds were given as gifts to kings and queens because of their reputation as a miracle food. **The Hindus, Arabs, Japanese, and Chinese have for centuries advocated the eating of almonds to enhance sexual potency and increase sexual virility.**

Almonds, unlike other nuts, which are acid forming, are alkaline. For sufferers of over-acid conditions of the stomach and even ulcers, almonds are the only nuts gentle enough not to cause a problem. These nuts are easily digested and are one of the most perfect foods on the Earth.

Almonds should always be eaten raw never roasted or salted and should be eaten in small quantities (6-10 at a time) for best results. Almonds can also be made into a milk in the following way:

Sweet Almond Milk

10 almonds
1 cup distilled water
1 tsp of honey or apple juice concentrate

Blend almonds and sweetener in water (in a blender) for a
    minute.
Pour over cereals in place of milk.

Eating a few almonds as a snack every couple of hours will provide sufficient nourishment to keep your blood sugar levels stable and help prevent over-eating at main meals. Almonds are an important addition to the diet for problems of menstrual irregularities, infertility, impotency, and prostate disorders as well as hypoglycemia, diabetes, arthritis, and uncontrollable hunger.

BEE POLLEN

Pollen is the fertile essence of mature flowers and is collected from the stamens of the blossoms by industrious bees. It takes approximately 40 hours to gather one tablespoon of pollen.

Bee pollen contains virtually every nutrient known, and it has gained the reputation of being a "super food." French agriculturist, Alain Caillas, concluded that 4 tablespoons of bee pollen a day would satisfy the total nutritional needs of the average person. Most athletes say that it improves their performance and gives them greater stamina and more energy.

Bee pollen contains all 22 amino acids, including the eight essential amino acids not manufactured by the body. It is very high in "Bee" vitamins and rich in all the essential minerals, including the hard to find trace minerals (see vitamin and mineral chapter).

Sexually speaking bee pollen is among the most incredible of foods. It contains **deoxiribosides** and **sterines,** plus steroid hormone substances. **Pollen also contains a gonadotrophic hormone, which is similar to the pituitary hormones FSH and LH that stimulate sex hormones of the ovaries and testes.** It is rich in aspartic acid and amino acid involved in rejuvenation of the sex glands. Rich in RNA, DNA, and superoxide dismutase (SOD), all anti-aging substances, **bee pollen is a youth-promoting food.**

Although bee pollen contains both male and female hormones, it is **higher in a testosterone-like hormone than in estrogen** and therefore is more successful in restoring the health of the male testes and in cases of prostate trouble than in correcting female hormonal imbalances. High in zinc as well as male hormones, pollen is a vital sexual rebuilder for man. Pollen is the mass of male germ cells which are collected from flowers. Bee pollen is not recommended for women because of its high content of male hormones. Taken in large quantities, it could upset the menstrual cycle. Women should refer to Royal Jelly for female hormonal support.

Bee pollen increases the body's own immunological function and stimulates and rejuvenates sex gland activity. In small amounts (one-quarter teaspoon a day) it can build immunity to pollen, a common allergy producing substance. In small amounts women can also take for allergy problems.

SUPPLEMENTATION WITH BEE POLLEN

Two capsules (local bee pollen) twice a day with meals or two teaspoons per day.

Footnote

Honey, sometimes referred to as the "nector of the Gods" is actually only a little better than refined sugars in terms of nutritional value.

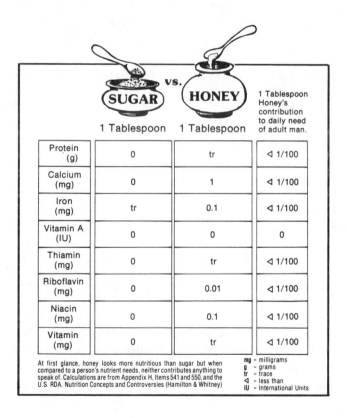

	SUGAR 1 Tablespoon	HONEY 1 Tablespoon	1 Tablespoon Honey's contribution to daily need of adult man.
Protein (g)	0	tr	◁ 1/100
Calcium (mg)	0	1	◁ 1/100
Iron (mg)	tr	0.1	◁ 1/100
Vitamin A (IU)	0	0	0
Thiamin (mg)	0	tr	◁ 1/100
Riboflavin (mg)	0	0.01	◁ 1/100
Niacin (mg)	0	0.1	◁ 1/100
Vitamin (mg)	0	tr	◁ 1/100

At first glance, honey looks more nutritious than sugar but when compared to a person's nutrient needs, neither contributes anything to speak of. Calculations are from Appendix H, Items 541 and 550, and the U.S. RDA. Nutrition Concepts and Controversies (Hamilton & Whitney)

mg = milligrams
g = grams
tr = trace
◁ = less than
IU = International Units

Russian scientists have discovered that **pollen is the active substance in honey resonsible for its rejuvenating properties.** The clean, clear honey sold in most stores is cooked and has all the pollen filtered out. **Natural, unstrained, unrefined, raw honey contains good amounts of pollen;** however, the simple sugar in honey is twice as sweet as refined sugar, hits the blood stream too quickly, and sticks to your teeth more readily than sugar. **Pollen, minus the honey, is a much better food.**

GARLIC

Garlic is as close to being a miracle medicine and food as you can get. Historically, used by the healthy Abkhazins of Russia, it has been called "Russian Penicillin" because of its extraordinary ability to fight infections of all types.

Such ailments as high blood pressure, diabetes, arthritis, cancer, asthma, allergies, intestinal worms parasitic diarrhea, and colds have been known to respond favorably to treatment with garlic.

In addition to containing allicin and alliin, substances which account for garlics antibacterial, anti-inflammatory, and antibiotic effects, garlic contains a very important trace mineral called selenium. Selenium, covered under the chapter "Vitamins & Minerals for Sex" is very important for sperm and semen production and optimum functioning of the prostate and testes.

The French, Italians, Spanish, and Mexicans all reported to have amorous and hot-blooded personalities have used garlic liberally in their cuisine for centuries. However, while garlic may increase sexual desire, it also keeps away vampires and other people. It is suggested that your sex partner also partake of garlic in order to insure complete compatibility. There are in the market some "odorless" garlic preparations, which can eliminate the problem of "garlic breath" if you find it too unappealing.

SUPPLEMENTATION WITH GARLIC

Eating two or three cloves of garlic or equivalent daily will help increase your **resistance** to infection and increase your **persistance** while making love. Two capsules three times a day with meals is another way to receive the benefits of this fantastic herb. **Kyolic**, an odorless garlic tablet, from Japan, is an excellent product.

Bon Appetit!

GINSENG

Ginseng is an ancient Chinese plant whose name is derived from the Chinese word, "genshen," meaning "man-roots" because it resembles the body of a man. The finger-thick root of ginseng frequently splits at the bottom and has side roots that make it look like the fingers of a man!

Ginseng root is an adoptogen, a substance that increases resistance to stress and strengthens the body's immune system. This root takes approximately seven to nine years to mature and Russia, China, Japan, and Korea are the main regions where ginseng crops are grown. True ginseng is a plant of the woodlakes, requiring rich, undisturbed soil in dense forests. Hundreds of years of harvesting have taken their toll on Oriental ginseng and the plant is virtually extinct in the world.

Russian research has established the following therapeutic functions of ginseng:

1. Lowering blood sugar (helpful in diabetes—dangerous for hypoglycemics).
2. Stimulates central nervous system.
3. Stimulates endocrine glands.
4. Increases hemoglobin (iron carrying part of blood).
5. Improves anemic condition.
6. Improves utilization of insulin in diabetic conditions.
7. Improves conditions of gastritis and hypertension.
8. Improves energy and elevates fatigue.
9. Improves sex drive.
10. Reduces blood cholesterol.

Scientists have discovered active ingredients in ginseng called **ginsenosides** which significantly alter the ability of the skeletal muscles to use free fatty acids rather than glucose for energy! **Ginseng also affects the adrenal glands as well as the hypothalamus and pituitary glands, presumably due to its steroid hormone-like qualities.** The hormone of ginseng have never been scientifically explored, yet the effect of these hormones seems to stimulate testosterone production of several capsules or several cups of tea are taken.

Producers of ginseng insist it is suitable for use by both sexes, yet in China, Dong Quai, another Chinese herb, is recommended by Chinese doctors for females, while ginseng is recommended for males. Dong Quai seems to possess female estrogen-like hormones and also stimulates their production in the body (see Dong Quai). I therefore, suggest ginseng for men and Dong Quai for women, unless ginseng is mixed with other female hormone producing herbs.

For therapeutic purposes **ginseng is helpful for increasing energy,** reducing fatigue, increasing endurance, stimulation of the endocrine system, and **particularly the male sexual organs and the adrenal glands**. It can be useful for people who must deal with stressful environmental situations and it is beneficial in male impotency and sterility problems. Ginseng also increases RNA and protein synthesis in the liver and aids the liver in cholesterol synthesis, which lowers cholesterol levels in the blood.

SUPPLEMENTATION WITH SIBERIAN GINSENG
(Males Only)

2 capsules with breakfast
2 capsules with lunch

Ginseng taken in the evening may produce insomnia.
Ginseng may be taken from time to time throughout a person's life as an energy booster.

164

DONG QUAI (Kwei)

The Chinese art of herbal healing has been extensively researched and many longevity herbs have been identified. Orientals for thousands of years have attributed rejuvenation and life extending power to Ginseng root and although this herb may be taken by both men and women, Chinese herbalists regard ginseng as a "man's herb."

The female equivalent of ginseng is another root called **Dong Quai**. The Chinese claim that Dong Quai has the remarkable ability to nourish female sex glands, rebuilding blood, and delays the symptoms of old age.

In youth the female sex glands, like those of the male, are healthy and active. **The vital sex hormones provided by healthy sex glands are directly related to the general health of the body and to the prolonged appearance of youth.**

In the female, beginning in the forties, a decline in hormonal output is partly responsible for the symptoms of aging. If the sex glands are nourished properly, these important sex hormones are once again produced at higher levels, resembling those levels produced by younger women. **An increase in diminished levels of sex hormones caused by aging would delay the symptoms of old age.**

Dong Quai is considered by Chinese healers to be helpful for correcting conditions of anemia as well as maintaining and improving the female hormones. Women in China use the herb once or twice a month for nourishing the sex glands.

METHOD OF PREPARATION

Place four cups of water in an enamel pan and add half a large Dong Quai root, cover loosely and bring to a boil. Simmer for several hours until liquid is only one and a half cups. Strain and drink broth warm.

SUPPLEMENTATION WITH DONG QUAI
(Females Only)

Find a source of Dong Quai from a local health food store in capsule or tablet form (preferably from China).

Two capsules twice a day until hormone condition is stabilized, then take twice a month if under 30. Women over 30, after hormonal sysmptoms are gone, should reduce the dosage to twice a week. Post-menopausal women may continue taking Dong Quai at a rate of 2 tablets a day.

2 capsules with breakfast
2 capsules with dinner

No hyperactive effects are noticed when taken in the evening.

Helps improve estrogen levels in premenopausal and postmenopausal women.

LICORICE

The ancient Chinese classified licorice a **first class** herb that preserved the life of man and could safely be taken in any amount.

Like the Chinese the Hindus considered licorice to be a general tonic, beautifying agent and elixir of life.

Licorice was found in the tombs of the Egyptian Pharaohs dating over 3,000 years ago.

Licorice is mentioned by Hippocrates, the father of medicine in 200 B.C. and used down through the ages for everything from asthma to menstrual difficulties. Licorice is mentioned in virtually all botanical records of mankind.

Down through the ages Licorice has been taken as a tea to purify the blood and to help neutralize acid conditions of the stomach.

Women have used licorice to keep them from becoming nauseous and sick during pregnancy. Licorice sooths coughs, hoarseness, and bronchial irritations. It helps loosen phlegm and lubricates the throat.

The licorice root yields a substance called **glycerhizin,** which is many times more sweet than cane sugar without the harmful side effects of refinded sugar (hypoglycemia and diabetes). **Licorice is often times recommended for hypoglycemics to help regulate the blood sugar levels.**

The root is one of the few herbs to contain a natural source of estrogen, a female sex hormone. In addition to the estrogen, licorice induce the adrenal cortex to produce larger amounts of cortisone and aldosterone for increased sexual energy. **Glycerhizin,** mentioned earlier, has similar chemical structure to that of **human steroid hormones.**

Licorice can be used successfully as a natural estrogen replacement for women who are menopausal or who are low in female sex hormones.

CAUTION

Large doses of licorice root should be avoided by those people with **high** blood pressure or **hyper**-adrenal function. Since licorice contains a substance similar to adrenal cortical hormones, extended large doses can also cause edema.

SUPPLEMENTATION WITH LICORICE ROOT

As a beverage — 1 tablespoon of root

Simmer for 15 minutes in 2 cups of distilled water
Drink 3 cups of beverage per day

Powder — 2 capsules twice a day with meals until symptoms subside.

OIL OF EVENING PRIMROSE

Indian medicine men treated everything from skin disease to asthma with a wild plant known as evening primrose (**Oenothera biennis**). When primrose oil was exported to Europe, it was known as **"the king's cure-all."** The oil, which is extracted from the seeds of evening primrose, contains a nutrient called gammalinolenic acid (GLA). **GLA has effects on prostaglandins which are very powerful, hormone-like substances presents in every cell of the human body.** Prostaglandin E, one form of prostaglandins, has been found to lower blood pressure, reduce cholesterol, increase female hormone production, and stimulate the immune system. GLA, the essential fatty acid in primrose oil, is a precursor of prostgaglandin E.

Studies done in England and Scandinavia on women with Premenstrual Syndrome (PMS) showed a decrease in breast pain, tenderness, heaviness, and lumps, as well as symptoms of depression, fluid retention, headaches, anxiety, anger, and irritability when they used primrose oil.

Oil of Primrose seems to regulate the function of the pituitary and hypothalamus which in turn regulates the sex hormones of the ovaries and uterus. Elevated **prolactin** levels, a sex hormone of the pituitary, can bring on PMS symptoms and enough PGE can reduce the amount of prolactin. Since primrose oil stimulates PGE, with gama-linolenic acid, the prolctin levels decrease and alleviate PMS symptoms.

SUPPLEMENTATION WITH OIL OF EVENING PRIMROSE

Two capsules twice a day (dosage should not exceed two grams a day).

Evening primrose oil is generally for women only. It can be helpful, however, in males who have symptoms of excess testosterone, psoriasis, eczema, acne, or other skin problems.

British and Canadian varieties of the oil seem to be the most potent and purest forms.

OLIVE OIL

Olive oil is the finest and most nutritious of all the vegetable oils available. It is mentioned many times in the Bible and has been used since ancient times in religious practices where "anointing" of the sick or establishing of priestly ordination was performed. Olive oil turns rancid very slowly because it is a monosaturated oil. Polyunsaturated oils, like corn, safflower, and peanut, turn rancid very quickly. Even exposure to light or increased temperatures can force these vegetable oils to become rancid. Rancidity in the human body can lead to the development of free radicals which are carcinogenic (cancer causing). Because olive oil is a monosaturated oil, when refrigerated, it will become like butter, while other vegetable oils will stay liquid. Olive oil is neither a polyunsaturated nor a saturated fat, giving it its unique quality of low risk of rancidity.

Rich in essential fatty acids, such as lineolic acid, olive oil provides substances necessary to build healthy sex glands and sex hormones. It contains a good amount of Vitamin E, which is helpful in increasing fertility. **Virgin olive oil, which is the first pressing** of the olives (only sesame and olive oil are pressed without heat or mechanical means), is the preferred oil. **Pure olive oil, although it sounds good, is not the first processing.** People of Latin countries, notorious for being hot lovers, include olive oil in their native dishes.

A combination of olive oil and lemon juice (garlic may be added) makes an excellent natural salad dressing. Olive oil is also excellent in soups or for sauteing.

Since ancient times, olive oil has been used by beautiful women around the world to feed and moisturize their skin and hair. Olive oil nourishes the skin and hair as well as keeping them from drying out.

BEFORE RETIRING

Rub one to two tablespoons of olive oil into hair and comb or brush in thoroughly. Place a shower cap over hair or place a towel over the pillow. Leave on overnight. Shampoo in the morning. Hair is lusterous and healthy after feeding with olive oil. Repeat as desired.

ROYAL JELLY

Royal jelly is a milky-white substance produced by pharyngeal glands of nurse bees and fed to the queen bee. This milky-like foodstuff contains 18 amino acids or building blocks of protein (amino acids are the components of sex hormones), including the eight essential amino acids. These amino acids include:

1.	Alanine	10.	Tyrosine
2.	Arginine	11.	Isoleucine*
3.	Aspartic acid	12.	Leucine*
4.	Proline	13.	Lysine*
5.	Glutonic acid	14.	Methionine*
6.	Glycine	15.	Phenylalanine*
7.	Histidine	16.	Threonine*
8.	Serine	17.	Tryptophan*
9.	Taurine	18.	Valine*

Royal Jelly is a storehouse of B vitamins. It is the richest natural source of pantothenic acid (B_5). The other eight vitamins included in this rich jelly are thiamine (B_1), riboflavin (B_2), niacin (B_3), pyridoxine (B_6), cabolamin (B_{12}), as well as biotin, folic acid, inositol, and choline. It also contains small amounts of Vitamins A, C, D, E, and calcium, iron, copper, phosphorus, silican, sulfur, and potassium, all nourishment for the endocrine glands and sex hormones.

Royal jelly has been used to treat rheumatoid arthritis, radiation poisoning, viral infections, psoriasis, eczema, burns, and diabetes. **No studies have ever shown any ill effects from use of the jelly.**

---

*Essential amino acid

Royal jelly consists of approximately three percent **unknown substances**, which means that it cannot be duplicated in a chemistry lab. It includes hormonal ingredients which account for the queen bee's fertility. **Royal jelly is a natural source of estrogen and pregesterone-like substances.**

Royal jelly is an excellent natural female hormone substitute for synthetic estrogen (synthetic estrogens can be cancer producing). Women who have had their ovaries surgically removed can use this product with positive results. Menopausal women also would benefit from royal jelly, and women who are attempting to correct infertility problems can help increase their estrogen/progesterone levels with royal jelly.

SUPPLEMENTATION WITH ROYAL JELLY

Royal jelly is very expensive but only a small amount is needed each day. A quantity equal to a rice kernel, placed under the tongue twice a day is sufficient. In capsule form, a dosage of two capsules a day is sufficient to obtain the desired results.

SARSAPARILLA

It is no accident that sarsaparilla became "rootbeer" and the Wild West has never been the same. Sarsaparilla contains natural testosterone and progesterone, thereby evoking increased sexual excitation. These male and female hormones keep the sex glands young and healthy. Sarsaparilla also contains **cortin**, an adrenal hormone which increases energy. **Pharmaceutical companies manufacture male and female sex hormone tablets from these hormones isolated in sarsaparilla.**

Sarsaparilla is a tropical plant found in Honduras, Mexico, and Ecuador. The root is the part utilized for medicinal purposes.

Sarsaparilla has been used for centuries for impotence.

Commercial rootbeer has no sarsaparilla in it so purchase the sarsaparilla root either in capsule form or in tea form.

SUPPLEMENTATION WITH SARSAPARILLA

2 capsules twice a day to increase libido or
1 teaspoon boiled for ten minutes in 2 cups of distilled
water, two or three times a day

SUNLIGHT AND SEXUAL HORMONES

We have migrated from an outdoor life on the farm into cities, where we spend most of our time in offices, houses, apartments and factories. **Indoor environment lighting provides one-tenth as much light compared to outdoor light in the shade!**

Sunlight affects sex hormone production by stimulating hormone secretion of the glands when (1) light passes through the pupil of the eye into the brain and (2) by producing hormones in the skin.

As light enters the pupil, nerves are stimulated in the back of the eye to transit impulses to the spinal cord. The impulses are sent back to the **pineal** gland in the brain. The hormone **melatonin**, produced by the pineal, stimulates the activity of the pituitary, hypothalamus, adrenals, ovaries and testes. **If the pineal doesn't receive enough light, it can stop ovulation and reduce estrogen production in a female.**

Male sex hormones are also elevated by sunlight. If the chest or back of a male is exposed to sunlight, male hormone production increases by 120 percent. When the genitals or testes are exposed to sunlight, the sexual hormones can increase by 200 percent.

Certain areas of the body when exposed to sunlight are more effective in stimulating hormone production than others. For instance, Vitamin D, a steroid hormone, is produced in greater quantities when the back rather than abdomen is exposed to sunlight. Sunlight produces sex hormones in the skin itself. Sunlight produces an estrogen-like substance in the skin which then is absorbed directly into the blood. This estrogen-like substance can produce a menstrual cycle in castrated female rats. In humans sunlight increases both female and male hormones significantly.

Women, with irregular periods, may develop regular, monthly cycles simply by several months of sunbathing and outdoor activities.

Perhaps modern society with its "shut-in" lifestyle is making men and women light starved. A sunlight starved person may develop sex dysfunction such as PMS, infertility, impotency and sterility.

Since the rays of the sun must pass through the pupils of the eyes in order to stimulate glandular brain activity, **glasses** are a **direct** hinderance to this vital process. **Sunglasses and corrective glasses block about 75 percent of sunlight out (five of seven parts of the spectrum).** If you must wear glasses, ask for ultraviolet transmitting plastic (UVR) to make your lenses. A few companies in the United States make full-spectrum lenses and one makes contacts.

For indoor use, companies are making full-spectrum natural flourescent lights which aid the skin and the eyes in absorbing the light it needs to function optimally. The company is:

Duro-Test Corporation
North Bergen, New Jersey

The name of this indoor light is called aptly, **Vita-Lite.**

SUNLIGHT AND WEIGHT LOSS

Farmers have known for many years that animals kept in the sun too much have difficulty in gaining weight. **Recent studies make it clear that sunlight does stimulate thyroid gland hormone production.** Since the thyroid gland regulates the basal metabolism rate, the rate at which you burn energy or calories, exposure to sunlight increases the basal metabolism rate and a person loses weight. Exercising in the sun would double the opportunity to lose unwanted weight.

SUNLIGHT AND CHOLESTEROL

Studies with both animals and humans demonstrate sunlight reduces cholesterol levels in the blood. Other studies indicate that exposure to sunlight lowers blood pressure and improves artherosclerosis. The safest time to be in sunlight is before 10:00 a.m. and after 4:00 p.m., although healthy cultures spend most of their lives outdoors at elevations of 5,000 to 7,000 feet above sea level and have no skin cancers. The relationship between skin cancer and sunlight is the relationship between high fat diets and sunlight. Since excess fat is stored in the tissues of the skin where sunlight can reach them, free radicals are more likely to be made. Free radicals have been demonstrated to cause cancers of various types. Something to think about!

*Read *Sunlight Could Save Your Life*, by Zane R. Kime, M.D., for all the scientific studies and research on this important topic.

A pastor was telling his flock about Solomon the Wise in the Bible, who had a thousand wives and concubines and fed them all ambrosia.

"Never mind what he _fed_ them", yelled a man out of the congregation, **"What did _he_ eat?"**

8

Exercise: Use It Or Lose It
Building Sexual Energy

"The secret of happiness is not in doing what one likes to do, but in liking what one has to do."
—Sir James M. Barrie

Out of 100 Americans:

> 43 don't have enough time
> 16 don't have the will power
> 12 don't feel like it
> 9 have medical reasons
> 8 lack energy
> 12 have some other excuse

Modern civilization, with its conveniences has brought with it less and less activity. Automobiles, buses, escalators, elevators, washing machines, television, office work and countless hours of sitting have transformed a once beautiful, graceful, erect, and slender sexually appealing body into the unattractive people of today. Rounded shoulders, poor muscle tone, pale faces, flabby underarms, thighs and waists, "pot bellies," stiff and inflexible joints, aching feet, and obesity are a few of the consequences of the inactivity of modern living.

A well-toned, energetic body is sexually attractive. Your body is poorly built for sitting and not much better for standing, but for walking, running and swimming, it is superb. **Many men have a heart attack while making love; could it be that they are so out of shape that the strain of sex kills them? You must be in physically good shape to have satisfying sex and a fit person is sexually appealing.**

The most important thing to remember in the beginning of an exercise program is that it is an essential to your health as eating, breathing, and sleeping. **Exercise releases the energy needed for other activities, including a satisfying sex life.**

If you permit your automobile to stand idle for a few years, the engine and body begin to corrode and rust. **Remember, too much rest brings rust. Action is a Law of Life.** Every organ, including the sexual organs, require activity in order to maintain strength, vitality, and virility, while stagnation will bring decay and death.

Exercise is crucial to the proper nutrition of the cells. Exercise is the primary way to circulate the nutrients in the blood in order to reach the trillions of cells in your body. If cells are not fed the proper foods and nutrients, and if these foods and nutrients are not delivered to them by sufficient and regular exercise, they become malnourished and die. Exercise also carries away the waste products of cellular metabolism so the cells don't rot in their own waste products.

To do any good, **exercise must be done at a level that will burn at least 2,000 excess calories a week and at a rate of exertion that will maintain a training heart rate.** To calculate your personal THR (training heart rate) use the following:

220 — Your Age = Maximum Heart Rate

Maximum Heart Rate × 65% = Training Heart Rate

AEROBIC EXERCISES

1. Steady, nonstop
2. Duration — 12 minutes **minimum**
3. Intensity — 65% of maximum heart rate

Four out of five Americans admit they're not getting enough exercise.

Just as a watch needs to be wound or leather polished, people need to work out to stay fit and flexible. Without physical activity, we become sluggish and dull, fat and sloppy. Stay sedentary and you can expect your energy to decrease, your sex life to become dull, and your temper to increase.

If you exercise regularly, what benefits can you expect?

1. Exercise helps keep your weight under control by burning extra calories.
2. Exercise keeps your muscles fit and trim.
3. Exercise reduces your risk of developing heart disease, obesity, arteriosclerosis, and high blood pressure by improving circulation and burning fat.
4. Exercise promotes relaxation.
5. Exercise reduces stress. **Action Absorbs Anxiety.**

Dr. Herbert DeVries, from the Gerontology Center of the University of Southern California, designed a study for volunteers between the ages of 52 and 70 who suffered from nervous tension. One group took 400mg of valium a day. The other group walked 15 minutes a day. This study demonstrated that walking was more effective than tranquilizers in relieving stress.

6. Exercise improves food digestion and speeds up a sluggish metabolism.

You are what you assimilate. Current studies suggest that regular exercise can increase your metabolism (rate at which you burn calories) up to thirty percent for two hours or more.

The bottom line in nutrition is to feed the cells of your body. Trillions of cells make up every organ, gland, and tissue. Cells digest and eliminate foods like you do. They are born, reproduce, and die. If they receive enough nutrients they will perform the appropriate functions. **Exercise is crucial to the proper nutrition of the cells.**

7. Exercise also increases your energy.
8. Allows you to spend quality time with yourself.
9. Gives you an opportunity to be outside.
10. Brings in more oxygen to every cell.
11. Improves sleep.
12. Reduces tendency to over-eat.
13. Allows you to meet new friends.
14. **Exercise increases your sexual energy.**

Some studies indicate that aerobic exercise decreases appetite by regulating your appestat, the brain center that controls appetite. These studies show that blood flow is redirected away from the digestive tract, stimulating the muscular use of blood fats instead of blood sugars. Unfortunately, the importance of somatopsychic physiology and medicine is not yet adequately appreciated.

Researchers at the University of Washington studied the health of 163 Seattle men between the ages of 25 to 75 who were victims of **sudden cardiac death**. Compared to community members who lived a sedentary lifestyle, the "vigorous" exercisers—those who spent more than 20 minutes a day walking, running, chopping wood, or swimming, had a 55 percent lower risk of sudden death. Mild or moderate levels of exercise—burning under 2,000 calories a week **did not lower the danger.**

Following are some of the aerobic exercises and the number of calories burned in an hour's workout. Remember, in order for exercise to be effective in reducing heart attack risks and improving circulation, you must burn 2,000 calories a week in your exercise program.

Exercise	Calories Per Hour
Running/Jogging	800-1,000
Walking	200-400
Swimming	500-700
Cross Country Skiing	700-900
Jumping Rope	300-600
Cycling	300-600
Rowing	800-1,000
Jazzercise	300-500

WALKING

Walking is probably the most natural and oldest form of exercise and certainly one of the best. Walking can be started at any age and maintained throughout your life. Because it is less strenuous than other forms of exercise, the chance of injury is less. While walking, almost all of your muscles are utilized, your abdominal muscles are tightened and strengthened, and you can experience permanent weight loss. You must burn 3,500 calories to lose one pound. A one hour walk every other day at a moderate pace (three miles per hour) will burn 300 to 400 calories; therefore, you can burn up a pound and a half a month or 18 pounds a year, providing you do not change your food intake. If you wish to lose weight faster, walk an hour a day, everyday and burn up three pounds a month or 36 pounds a year.

MINI-TRAMPOLINE

Utilization of the small trampoline (sometimes called a mini-trampoline) designed for home or office use is an excellent way to exercise indoors. Although you should not expect to lose much weight from "rebounding," jumping and jogging on your rebounder stimulate circulation, heart rate and elimination. You can listen to music or watch your favorite television program while you jump. Half an hour, twice a day, is ideal to improve your energy and health.

JOGGING

To "jog" literally means to "jar." Subjecting your body to a daily regime of pounding on asphalt or cement, thereby bruising kidneys, liver, reproductive organs, knees, lower back and ankles, does not sound like a way to maintain good health.

Instead, find a beautiful park, country road or golf course where you can run on grass or dirt. This practice reduces the stress on the muscular/skeletal system, as well as the kidneys. Warm up by stretching ten minutes before you run and cool down with stretching exercises for 20 minutes afterwards to reduce the possibility of sprains and other injuries caused by shortening muscles. The proper shoes will help absorb **some** of the shock of jogging.

SWIMMING

Lap swimming is an excellent aerobic endurance workout. However, do not expect to lose much weight as the body will retain fat in order to maintain body heat in the water. Swimmers have a larger percentage of body fat than any other aerobic exerciser. If possible, avoid chlorinated pools.

CYCLING

Cycling can be a fine aerobic exercise if done on a lap basis like swimming. Unfortunately, many people "coast" a significant amount of the time while riding, resulting in a little actual exercise. For maximum results, find a bike path or park where you can build up speed for a continuous amount of time.

JUMPING ROPE

This form of exercise, like rebounding, is an excellent winter or year-round indoor sport. If possible, jump on a thick rug or mat to minimize muscular/skeletal system jarring.

ROWING

Regular use of a rowing machine is an excellent way to exercise the entire body—arms, back, legs, chest, and stomach. Rowing is perhaps the finest all-around fitness exercise.

CONCLUSION

The greatest pick-me-up is not a cup of coffee or candy bar, but **exercise**. Exercise makes you feel good all over and relieves tension, too. Most of our lives are so full of stress that exercise becomes an essential ingredient to relieve the resultant tension. Exercise is also a great remedy for depression, anxiety, and worry.

Exercise boosts your energy level for at least two hours, making it a prescription for fatigue. **A tired person isn't interested in sex.** A person needs energy to enjoy sexual activity and exercise is a wonderful Elixir for sexual energy.

Besides aerobic exercise, including stretching and flexibility exercises as part of your daily program. Hatha Yoga, which is a system of ancient exercise techniques for stretching and breathing, is an excellent method of toning up the sexual organs, the lungs and the nervous system. People who have low sexual energy or are under a lot of stress and strain will derive great value from practicing a few Yoga postures.

Exercise will permit blood to circulate freely from the top of your head to the tips of your toes. All the sex glands will receive the protein, carbohydrates, fats, vitamins, and minerals they need through proper circulation of the blood. **Exercise improves digestion and insures, coupled with the OH! YES! diet, a healthy sex life.**

CAUTION: SEE YOUR PHYSICIAN BEFORE BEGINNING ANY EXERCISE PROGRAM.

9

Tune-Up Your Sex Life:
Fasting For Rejuvenation

"Better keep yourself clean and bright; you are the window through which you must see the world."
—George Bernard Shaw

The practice of fasting is at least as old as the many fasts recorded in the Bible. Abraham fasted, Moses fasted, Daniel fasted, and even the Son of God, Jesus, fasted. Records of fasting for spiritual cleansing are in all the ancient texts. Egyptians, Chinese, Hebrews, Greeks, and Hindus have utilized fasting as a means of denying the earthly or physical needs or passions in order to commune with their Creator. Fasting for rejuvenation of the organs and glands of the body is another excellent purpose for fasting.

A "higher purpose" for fasting has sometimes been replaced by a "lower purpose," vanity. Many men and women fast not for spiritual reasons, nor for health reasons, but simply to lose weight. **Fasting to achieve quick weight loss is as unhealthy for you as smoking to lose weight.** A slow, progressive weight loss (two pounds a week) is the healthiest and safest way to experience permanent weight loss. Dropping fifteen to forty pounds in a month or six weeks damages the endocrine glands, the sex hormones, and the metabolism. **Such a quick, unhealthy, weight loss leaves a person's body starved, depleted, and exhausted.** The metabolism becomes so sluggish after such a marathon fast that severe sugar cravings (brain and Nervous system are

185

starved) and over-eating are the result. **STARVING IS NOT FASTING.**

PROPER FASTING

Of all of Nature's techniques for healing your body, fasting is one of the most effective. Eliminating **solid food** in lieu of liquid food permits the body to use the energy normally required for digestion, for self-regeneration. The therapeutic effect of fasting has been documented by many years of clinical experience both in Europe and in the United States.

In addition to fasting for the obvious benefit of correcting and healing imbalances and even diseases in the body, many people around the world fast regularly, not to cure any particular ailment, but to cleanse their bodies. These people consider fasting an excellent means for removing accumulated modern living. **Fasting also increases stamina and resistance against illness or disease and will revitalize all the vital organs of the body, including the sex organs. Fasting will help renew your sexual energy and make you appear younger.**

Periodic short fasts (three days to a week) perform a tune up on all the **sex glands and sex organs.** Properly done, fasting will result in feelings of physical, mental and spiritual invigoration. **Fasting actually charges and refreshes you with new-found sexual energy.** Fasting will remove the waste products of your body, resulting in a cleaner complexion. Fasting is a physical "house cleaning" that helps you lose extra pounds while toning the entire system (especially the sexual organs). **Fasting is an opportunity for a "new beginning," an opportunity to recuperate, renew, and regroup lost energy and health.**

There are special and scientific ways not only to fast, but also to prepare for and break a fast. **Fasting done incorrectly and for the wrong reasons can be dangerous and unhealthy.**

WHAT TO DRINK

Raw fruit juices like apple juice, orange juice, grape juice, pineapple juice, and grapefruit juice are excellent providers of needed natural sugar to keep the blood sugar and energy level up. Raw vegetable juices like carrot juice, celery juice, beet juice, and green drinks made from alfalfa, comfrey, carrot and beet tops, parsley, wheat grass or other fresh greens provide the vitamins and minerals in an easily digestible form for the entire body. Fresh fruit and vegetable juices are excellent sources of amino acids (protein), enzymes, vitamins, minerals, and trace minerals required to build up the sex organs while giving the digestive organs a well deserved rest. In order to insure that fruit and vegetable juices are fresh, prepare them in an electric juicer just before drinking during the duration of your fast.

Another important beverage used in many European fasting clinics is vegetable broth. In Dr. Paavo Airola's book, *How to Keep Slim, Health, and Young with Juice Fasting,* (Health Plus Publishers, Phoenix, AZ), an excellent recipe for a potassium-rich broth is given:

VEGETABLE BROTH

2 large potatoes, unpeeled, chopped or sliced to
   approximately one-half inch pieces
1 cup carrots, shredded or sliced
1 cup red beets, shredded or sliced
1 cup celery, leaves and all, chopped to one-half inch
   pieces
1 cup any other available vegetables: beet tops, turnips
   and turnip tops, parsley, cabbage or a little of everything.

Use stainless steel, enameled or earthenware utensil. Fill it up with one and one-half quarters of water and slice the vegetables directly into the water to prevent oxidation. Do not peel potatoes, beets or carrots. Just brush them well. Cover and cook slowly for at least a half hour. Let stand for another half hour; strain, cool until warm and serve. If not used immediately, keep in refrigerator. Warm it up before serving.

A short fast does not require stopping normal work or other activities, but you must avoid **over-strenuous** physical or mental work. Walking a half hour to an hour each day of the fast is in order to cleanse the blood and organs of waste products as well as to invigorate the body with an additional supply of oxygen.

GENERAL SUGGESTIONS

Since one-third of the wastes eliminated during a fast are eliminated through the skin, adequate bathing, especially in conjunction with a **dry brush** massage is helpful (dry brush can be purchased from Jensen Products or from health food stores.) Sufficient liquid intake, up to a gallon, including fruit and vegetable juices, broth, and distilled or spring water, will assist the kidneys in removing waste products. Adding one tablespoon of flax seeds and one tablespoon of raw wheat bran soaked over night in vegetable broth once or twice a day will provide a natural, mild laxative to assist the bowels in normal peristalsis to eliminate accumulated wastes. Daily warm water enemas, which will facilitate removal of toxins and other wastes during each day of a fast, are an absolute must according to Dr. Airola.

SCHEDULE FOR EACH DAY OF FASTING

1. Upon rising take an enema
2. Dry brush massages before a warm and cool alternating shower
3. Breakfast: hot vegetable broth drink
4. Walk 30 minutes to one hour
5. Between Meals: fresh fruit or vegetable juices diluted fifty-fifty with distilled water
6. Lunch: hot vegetable broth drink
7. Between Meals: more fruit or vegetable juices

8. Dinner: hot vegetable broth drink
9. Retire early after a quiet evening of spiritual reading

For a detailed program of do-it-yourself juice fasting, read Dr. Airola's book, *How to Keep Slim, Healthy, and Young with Juice Fasting.*

It is best to start with a one to three day fast before attempting to fast for longer periods. Preparation for and breaking of a short fast are not as important as for a longer fast, although eating lightly before and after any length fast is recommended.

Dr. Airola's juice fasting program may be adapted for a working person. **Consulting a physician before undergoing any fast longer than three days is always advisable.**

10

For Women Only!

"A perfect woman, nobly plann'd,
To warn, to comfort, and command;
And yet a spirit still, and bright
With something of an angel-light."
—William Wordsworth

PMS — PRE-MENSTRUAL SYNDROME

Queen Victoria was known to go into "royal rages" monthly, unless pregnant. Honest Abe Lincoln probably honestly wished Mary Todd Lincoln would go away during certain phases of her menstrual cycle because, according to reports, she was irritable, unreasonable, angry, and depressed. These women and millions of others before and since, have suffered through a time each month which husbands, boyfriends, children, friends, and they themselves wish didn't have to occur. Today this is referred to as **premenstrual syndrome (PMS).**

PMS affects about 40 percent of all American women between the ages of 18 to 45 to some degree. The symptoms can begin ten days before and continue several days after menstruation, leaving millions of women feeling poorly for half of every month. The following list of symptoms is common:

THE SYMPTOMS OF PMS

PSYCHOLOGICAL

irritability
anxiety
loss of concentration
depression
insomnia
changes in sex drive
nervous tension

aggression
crying spells
mood swings
forgetfulness
mental confusion
fatigue

PHYSICAL

weight gain
headaches
swelling
joint pain
increased appetite
acneseness
water retention

hoarseness
migraines
breast tenderness
cramps
constipation
sugar cravings
bloating

Depending on symptoms, women may fall into one or more categories:

Anxiety
nervous tension
mood swings
anxiety
irritability

Craving
headache
craving sweets
insomnia
increased appetitie
heart pounding
dizziness/fainting

Depression
depression
forgetfulness
confusion
crying

Hyperhydration
weight gain
swelling of extremities
breast
tenderness
fatigue

The proper balance of estrogen produced in the follicles of the ovaries is coordinated by the appropriate timing of the hypothalamic stimulation of the pituitary gland. The pituitary's production of FSH and LH insures a smooth ovulation during which time progesterone is produced. Progesterone helps regulate the duration of the menstrual cycle. **Medical experts have established that PMS is an imbalance of hormones in a woman's body which begins sometime prior to the menstrual cycle.** Hormonal imbalances can improve or become worsened by the foods a woman eats. The "Standard American Diet" or S.A.D. is devoid of the vitamins and minerals needed to permit a woman's body to function well, includin the time before, during and after menstruation. **When proper nutrition is not provided, the undernourished endocrine glands cannot produce the proper mixture of sex hormones needed for regular, pain-free premenstrual and menstrual function.**

Women who want to correct both the symptoms of PMS and hormonal imbalances of estrogen and progesterone must eliminate the hormone suppressing foods and beverages covered in the chapter on **"Unsexy Foods: Full but Famished"** and summarized below.

"Foods" That Aggravate PMS

1. Refined sugars and fats
2. Processed and refined foods
3. Caffeine (coffee, tea, pop, chocolate)
4. Alcohol
5. High protein foods
6. Saturated fats (dairy products and red meats)

All the above "foods" rob the body of valuable nutrients and upset hormonal balance.

Refined Sugar—depletes needed B vitamins, especially B$_6$ needed for proper hormonal and sodium/potassium fluid balances. It also depletes calcium and magnesium needed to decrease cramps, stabilize the blood sugar and keep nerves calm. It increases cravings for sweets and empty starches as well as causing headaches, mood swings, and irritability.

Dairy Products—loaded with salt will produce water retention. High in fat, blocks liver metabolism of estrogen. Pasteurized milk and cheese interfere with metabolism of calcium and magnesium.

Caffeine—increases irritability. Depletes B complex and increases breast tenderness. Chocolate intensifies sweet cravings and depletes B complex, calcium, and magnesium.

Alcohol—robs the body of B complex vitamin and calcium/magnesium. Toxic to the liver and therefore the liver cannot reduce levels of estrogen in the blood.

Beef, Pork, and Lamb—high fat content reduces liver efficiency, depletes zinc, calcium, and magnesium. Synthetic estrogen hormones can upset menstruation.

Strict adherence to the **"OH! YES! Diet"** and the supplementation listed below should improve symptoms of PMS in approximately three to six months.

With Meals

Vitamin E—alpha-tocopherols—400 I.U. twice a day
Vitamin C—calcium ascorbate—1000mg twice a day
Vitamin A—beta carotene—10,000 units twice a day
Vitamin B-Complex—(50mg each, rice based)—2 tablets
    twice a day
Vitamin B_6—(rice based)—50mg twice a day
Zinc Chelate—50mg once a day
Magnesium Chelate or Orotate—200mg twice a day
Licorice Root—1 capsule twice a day
Vitamin F—1 capsule twice a day
Calcium Chelate or Orotate—800mg before sleep only
Oil of Primrose—2 capsules once a day
Dong Quai—1 tablet a day

PMS Foods: Whole grains, vegetables, fruits, almonds, sunflower seeds, avocados, salmon and other fin and scale fish, plain low-fat yogurt. Read "Sexy Foods: **OH! YES! Diet.**"

ADDITIONAL CONSIDERATIONS

ORAL CONTRACEPTIVES AND PMS

Birth-control pills, containing synthetic compounds of progesterone and estrogen, **inhibit** the hypothalamus and pituitary glands from secreting FSH and LH and consequently **prevent** ovulation. Pill users learn the hard way that infertility and increased menstrual problems often occur after they stop taking The Pill. "Over-suppression syndrome" is a term created to explain what synthetic estrogen and progesterone in oral contraceptives have done to upset or even stop the normal secretion of sex hormones by the pituitary, hypothalamus, and ovaries needed or the natural cycle of menstruation. Depending on the health of the glands before taking oral contraceptives as well as the length of time (one, two, or ten years) they are taking escalation of the **post-pill problems** of amenorrhea (absence of menstrual periods), irregular menstruation, infertility, and sterility occurs.

THYROID AND PMS

There is evidence that a sluggish thyroid (hypothroidism) contributes to PMS symptoms; women with an underactive thyroid are more likely to suffer from PMS. If you suffer from such symptoms as dry skin, weight gain, irritability, constipation, feeling cold, fatigue, and sweet cravings, hypothyroidism may be involved in your PMS. Undergoing T_3 and T_4 thyroid blood test from your medical doctor will tell you if your thyroid is functioning normally. Even though the "normal" range for thyroxin is from 4.0 to 13.00 on a T_4 test, even "low normals" from 4.0 to 6.5 on a T_4 test could produce symptoms of hypothyroidism. Women with hypothyroidism are often treated with synthetic thyroid hormones which do not correct the thyroid's poor functioning.

A combination of nutritious foods (proper feeding of the thyroid), exercise (to stimulate thyroid activity), supplementation as suggested earlier in this chapter, shoulder stands (yoga), the elimination of excess iodine in the diet (table and sea salt products), and the addition of a whole thyroid gland (protomorphogens) bought at a natural foods store will help stimulate the sluggish thyroid to begin producing more thyroxin.

STARVATION DIETS AND PMS

Another modern day problem contributing to PMS is the preoccupation of American women to be thin. A lack of sufficient calories in a woman's daily diet will not produce enough carbohydrate, protein and fat in the body to assist in glandular function and subsequent estrogen and progesterone production. Many cases of amenorrhea and PMS have been corrected by a diet of natural foods (2,000-2,500 calories per day) in combination with certain supplements. Anorexic women, models, gymnasts, and athletes who register a low percentage of body fat (4-10%) also report irregular or no periods. Fat cells make an important contribution to the normal production and distribution of sex hormones. Young girls do not start menstruation **until** they reach a critical body weight. Under-weight girls and women develop irregular and infrequent periods because not enough estrogen is produced. Overweight women with excesses of estrogen are more prone to cancer, diabetes, heart and gall bladder disease, as are Premarin (synthetic estrogen) users.

In healthy cultures, women average around 20 percent body fat and a daily calorie intake of 2,500 to 3,500. Their ovulation, periods, and disposition are regular, predictable, and mild. They do not have any of the symptoms of PMS. They eat only whole grains, vegetables, fruits, nuts, and seeds, a little yogurt, and even less meat, poultry, and fish. They do not indulge in sweets, processed or refined foods, fried foods, caffeine, or diet pop. Due to their low-salt intake, healthy women have no pre-menstrual swelling of the face, ankles, or abdomen. If you are under or overweight, check the life insurance tables and establish a weight within ten pounds on either side of the numbers indicated for your height, frame size, and age. To insure an optimum weight with sufficient body fat to produce proper sex hormones, follow the recommendations outlined in this book in the chapter called "Sexy Foods: **OH! YES! Diet.**"

ENDOMETRIOSIS

Endometriosis is a condition in which endometrial cells, of which the lining of the uterine consists, start growing outside the uterus, in the pelvic cavity. This sticky, clotted tissue, which reacts to the hormonal cycle and is stimulated by estrogen, adheres to the intestines, ovaries, and fallopian tubes.

Endometriosis is a major cause of abdominal cramps, menstrual pain, and even infertility. This sticky, clotted tissue creates cysts and lesions that drain, producing appendicitis type pain. Endometriosis is commonly observed during hysterectomy even though most of the time it was not previously diagnosed. Endometriosis tends to come and go according to the estrogen levels.

These misplaced endometrial cells, unlike the uterine linings, grow outside the uterus and therefore are not discharged during normal menstrual periods. These tissues continue to grow and proliferate in the pelvic cavity. Hemorrhage is common and other symptoms frequently experienced are rectal pain during periods, menstrual irregularities, tenderness in the abdomen followed by cramping prior to periods, burning pain in the ovaries and infertility caused by endometrial tissue growing on the ovary, blocking ova and also choking off fallopian tubes.

Endometriosis covers a wide range of symptoms from excessive bleeding during menstruation to complete stoppage of periods. Hormonal imbalances are found in practically all forms of this problem. Some authorities believe I.U.D.'s and oral contraceptives are the major culprits in endometriosis. Other authorities assert that poor nutrition causes an imbalance of estrogen production and disturbs the uterine lining. When endometriosis develops, the uterus becomes inflamed, tender, swollen and of a spongy texture.

One thing is certain, estrogen causes the condition to worsen. Most treatments involve suppressing the estrogen supply or in severe cases, a complete hysterectomy (removal of ovaries and uterus) is suggested.

Another alternative "cure" is pregnancy, since during pregnancy, the predominant hormone produced is progesterone, which depresses estrogen production. The lowering of estrogen production has a positive effect on endometriosis. Synthetic male hormones or synthetic progesterone can create an artificial pregnancy or menopause, thus relieving symptoms of endometriosis. Since endometriosis can lead to endometrial cancer and ovarian cancer, this problem is not harmless, painless, or without consequences. However, surgical or chemical neutering are not often necessary.

Less dangerous and harmful than drugs and surgery is the health power of good nutrition, supplementation, and fitness, **unless** severe disease is involved.

In my consulting practice I have found that women who develop endometriosis are usually internally tense, overly stressed, self-critical, perfectionists, dieters, junk food eaters, and diet pop drinkers. Some also attempt self-medication through aspirin or other drugs to relax their stressful lives.

Starvation diets, downing several cans of diet pop a day and in some cases anorexic behavior, coupled with a lot of social, professional, financial, and personal pressure can initiate or worsen endometriosis.

Nutritionists have known for years that hormone levels are dependent upon the foods eaten. What you eat can modify estrogen levels. Estrogen is necessary before and during ovulation and the progesterone should help lower estrogen levels to stop ovulation. Although no specific cause is known for endometriosis, estrogen accelerates its development. Women with endometriosis seem to produce estrogen not only during menstruation, but at other times of the month as well. Perhaps a faulty liver is part of the problem since the liver is the site of estrogen breakdown. If nutrition is adequate, particularly in B Complex vitamins, the liver will eliminate excess estrogen (see chapter on vitamins and minerals). All grains are full of B vitamins (chapter on Sexy Food) but **whole wheat contains estrogen-like compounds that may increase estrogen output in women.** Eliminate wheat for three months to see if improvement is noted. Cirtrus, rich in biofavonoids, which are similar to estrogen, can aggravate endometriosis. Eliminate oranges and grapefruits from your diet for three months. Alcohol as well as refined sugar and excessive prolonged stress depletes B vitamins. One of the first symptoms of B vitamin depletion is painful periods and low B vitamins allow estrogen to assimilate in the body.

Along with the B vitamins, inositol, and choline help to maintain liver function. Recent studies indicate that B_6, taken with magnesium, helps to reduce estrogen build up in some women. Calcium is related to estrogen production and vice versa, while magnesium regulates the production of progesterone. Remember, progesterone lowers estrogen levels to regulate ovulation. Vitamin E helps correct uterine disorders and reduce breast cysts, both of which are related to excess estrogens. Also, Vitamin E helps heal scar tissue and minimize adhesions: moderate exercise helps normalize hormone levels. Also, regular exercise reduces and releases stress which contributes to development of endometriosis (see chapter on Exercise).

Nutrition, supplementation, and exercise will not correct any condition, especially a hormonal imbalance, quickly. **Neither Rome, nor your body, was built in a day, so be patient. Six months is a good time frame in which to expect results.** Initially, a worsening of symptoms of endometriosis will be experienced since stimulated glands will produce more estrogen, but in time, the liver will break down the estrogen when the ovaries produce it.

Always try nature before drugs and surgery are employed.

SYMPTOMS OF ENDOMETRIOSIS

Bloating
Abdominal pain
Swollen abdomen
Ovarian pain
Severe and extreme menstrual bleeding
Rectal pain
Burn sensations in Fallopian tubes
Infertility
Irregular ovulation

SUPPLEMENTATION

All with Meals:

> B-Complex (rice based) — 100mg/3x/day
> B_6 — 50mg/3x/day
> Magnesium Chelate — 200mg/3x/day
> Choline — 750mg a day
> Inositol — 400mg a day
> Vitamin E — 400 I.U./2x/day
> Vitamin C (Calcium ascorbate) — 1000mg/2x/day

The **OH! YES! Diet** of nutrition with the exception of wheat products, dairy products, and citrus products is advised. Eliminate **all** unsexy foods (see chapter). Moderate, regular exercise is vital for stress reduction and proper digestion and assimilation of food and vitamins.

MENOPAUSE AND OSTEOPOROSIS

Change of Life, or menopause, means the end of the reproductive capacity of a female. It can occur as early as the thirties but usually menopause occurs between the ages of forty and fifty.

The symptoms of Menopause are:

Hot flashes
Osteoporosis (brittle bones)
Calcium metabolism imbalances
Hot sweats
Sexual disinterest
Irritability
Insomnia
Mental Instability
Depression
Hormone depletion

Although menopause cannot be avoided through appropriate health habits, for several years, when it does occur, many of the unpleasant symptoms and degenerative consequences can be avoided altogether.

Since menopause often has a profound effect on a woman's personality as well as her body, leaving her mentally unstable as well as subjected to osteoporosis, the following suggestions of diet and supplementation should be carefully practiced by all women who wish to maintain their vitality.

A woman is especially vulnerable to calcium depletion during menstruation and if she doesn't replace her calcium loss, osteoporosis can begin to develop, even before menopause. Calcium replacement is vital for all menstruating women and becomes increasingly important during menopause.

Calcium levels in the blood are regulated by hormones, particularly estrogen. During menopause, the hormonal activity slows down as reproductive age diminishes and calcium requirements are not met.

The skeleton is a storehouse for calcium and during the normal physiological, biological, and biochemical processes carried on by the body, calcium is in and out of the bones (over 90% of all the calcium in the body is stored in the bones).

Many people think their bones reach a certain size and shape at adulthood and remain stagnant and hard during the course of their lives. Actually the bones are in a continual state of flux, changing constantly growing and repairing themselves. The skeleton acts as a reservoir for storage of calcium and phosphorus, which in turn carries on hundreds of metabolic and physiological functions in order to maintain homeostasis.

When the loss of calcium in the bones exceeds the gain, a thinning of the bones begins. The techniques for measuring bone loss are not precise enough to establish one number, but instead, a range of numbers indicate susceptibility to fractures. An unhealthy man or woman could lose up to 40 percent of his or her skeleton without coming into that "fracture range." By the time osteoporosis is diagnosed, significant and advanced stages of bone loss have already occurred.

Actually, thousands of people break their hips (or their hips break and then they fall—it can't always be determined which comes first) and hundreds of thousands suffer from broken ankles, wrists, arms, curvature of the spine, and fractures of the vertebrae. **Since it is easier to prevent a disease than to cure a disease**, there are better strategies for preventing osteoporosis than for rebuilding bones.

A growing number of TV commercials and magazine ads seek to oversimplify the problem of osteoporosis with the promotion of a single nutrient, calcium, and usually in poorly assimilate forms. About two-thirds of bone consists of calcium, phosphorous, and magnesium, with traces of sodium, zinc, lead, and other elements. These nutrients form fibers which form crystals that bind tightly with a protein known as **collagen**. Healthy bone is stronger than steel and reinforced concrete, but take away the minerals and the collagen, and bones become inflexible. The bone becomes so brittle it can crumble into dust. Vitamin C plays an invaluable part in preserving the healthy collagen that surrounds the bone. Bone and collagen degeneration are accelerated because of the lack of sufficient Vitamin C in the Standard American Diet (S.A.D.)

Since osteoporosis has become epidemic in the last thirty-five years, perhaps a closer look at a typical "modern" diet will shed some light on the course of bone degeneration.

Hormones influence the metabolic process that feed calcium and phosphorous into the bone structure in proper proportions. How well these minerals and others reach the bones determines whether the gain/loss can be kept in balance.

Dietary Phosphorous and Calcium should be approximately the same proportion or 1 to 1 (some authorities recommend a 2 to 1 calcium to phosphorous ratio) in order for the body to absorb both minerals properly. The S.A.D. contributes to calcium depletions and osteoporosis by supplying an excess of phosphorous. Meat, for instance, contains 22 times more phosphorous than calcium, and serious malabsorption of calcium results. High protein foods like beef, pork, veal, lamb, and poultry provide Americans with an abundance of phosphorous with calcium becoming a victim of neglect. Many dieticians and doctors just advocate drinking more milk and eating more dairy products to increase calcium intake. However, the fact that calcium and magnesium deficiencies as well as osteoporosis are so widespread in Americans of all ages, especially the elderly and post-menopausal women, may be explained by an examination of cow's milk versus human milk.

RATIO OF MINERALS

COW'S MILK TO HUMAN MILK

Calcium . . . . 3.57 to 1
Magnesium . . . . 3.35 to 1
Phosphorous . . . . 6.25 to 1
Potassium . . . . 2.23 to 1
Sodium . . . . 3.12 to 1

*U.S. Department of Agriculture

It would be all right to have higher concentrations of minerals in cow's milk, but it's the much higher ratio of phosphorous in proportion to calcium that bothers researchers. Diets high in phosphorous increase calcium and magnesium requirements.

Many authorities argue that the average American doesn't get enough calcium to protect the bones. **Instead of attempting to elevate calcium levels in order to keep up with a high phosphorous diet, perhaps the solution can be found in returning to the foods eaten by healthy cultures.** These people around the world who are healthy, virile, and show very little osteoporosis, even in ages over a hundred, eat very little dairy and meat (see **Sexy Foods: OH! YES! Diet**).

The dietary recommendations for pre and post-menopausal women would be to eat a diet free of all processed, refined, and denatured foods and an abundance of whole, nautral grains, seeds, and nuts, rich in Vitamin E, and minerals like calcium, magnesium, phosphorous (in proper balance) and zinc. Consult the **OH! YES! Diet** for specific instructions.

Since a woman who is not pregnant requires less protein than a woman who is, a significant reduction in beef, pork, veal, and poultry high in phosphorous would assist the body in absorbing more calcium, zinc, and magnesium for proper bone development.

SUPPLEMENTATION FOR MENOPAUSE AND OSTEOPOROSIS
(Use After Hysterectomy Also)

Vitamin E — d-alpha-tocopherols — 400 I.U. twice daily
    (stimulates estrogen production)
B_6 — 50mg twice daily (rice based)
B-Complex — 50mg twice daily
Vitamin C — calcium ascorbate — 2000mg twice daily
Primrose Oil — 2 capsules twice daily
Licorice Root — 2 capsules twice daily
Magnesium Chelate — 500mg in the morning before
    breakfast
Calcium Chelate — 1000mg at bedtime only
Betaine Hydrochloride — 1 tablet after each meal
    (facilitates calcium absorption)

Vitamin A — beta carotene — 10,000 I.U. twice a day
Zinc Chelate — 50mg a day
Dong Quai — 1 tablet twice daily
Vitamin F — 2 capsules twice a day

These supplement recommendations satisfy the lowered hormonal balance caused by a partial or complete hysterectomy. The use of synthetic estrogen replacement is not recommended since they may lead to the formation of cancers in the body. A partial hysterectomy does not permit the ovaries to function properly even though women are told they do.

INFERTILITY

In 1982, almost half of all American married couples with wives in the childbearing ages were sterile or had some childbearing impairment. While eight million were voluntarily sterilized, another 6.3 million were unable or unlikely to have additional births. These related statistics on infertility in the U.S. are from the National Survey of Family Growth conducted by the National Center for Health Statistics.

In 1982, about 6.3 million married women, 15-44 years of age had used infertility services at some time. **Perhaps there are several million more women in the United States for financial, personal, or other reasons never used official infertility services.** Perhaps many of these "non-statistically" infertile women solved the problem nutritionally themselves or were counseled by a professional nutritionist.

Infertility is a very real problem in the United States and millions of women have to face the possibility of never being physically able to bear children.

Most authorities in the field of infertility place poor and irregular ovulation, drugs and oral contraceptives as the most common causes of infertility.

I suggest to any woman who wishes to have a child at anytime in her life that she stop using licit or illicit drugs, avoid caffeine, alcohol, smoking, and oral contraceptives.

The **OH! YES! Diet** will improve a woman's fertility and the supplementation recommendations in the PMS section of this chapter will not only stabilize ovulation, but also improve the chances of pregnancy, unless contraception is used.

11

For Men Only!

"What a disgrace it is for a man to grow old without ever seeing the beauty and strength of which his body is capable."

—Socrates

IMPOTENCE AND STERILITY

Impotence and sterility are at an all-time high in the United States, even among younger men. The average sperm count of American men has been declining significantly in the last fifty years. In 1929, studies show American men averaged 100 million sperm per cubic centimeter of semen. Today the average count is only 60 million.

Impotence is related to sexual performance (the inability to achieve or maintain an erection) and **sterility** is related to low sperm count. Sexual performance can be adequate even in sterile men, and impotent men may have a normal sperm count. **Both of these imbalances are very much related to dietary and physiological causes, and they have similar treatments.**

Most doctors would not tell a sterile man that his problem is psychological and that he should see a psychiatrist. And yet psychiatrists often blame impotence on inhibitions, feelings of inadequacy, fear of failure, and unusual sexual demands by liberated women. All of these are valid factors, but medicine should not look for psychosomatic causes unless and until they have ruled out nutritional deficiences and dietary imbalances. **Fear of failure becomes**

psychological after several failures, which are more often than not originated as the result of physical and dietary inadequacies.

Following are a list of physical causes of both impotence and sterility.

1. **Drugs** — antihypertensive, tranquilizers, cinetidine (known as Tagamet for ulcers), marijuana, cocaine, and even aspirin.

Prescription, non-prescription, and recreational drugs all have one thing in common—all have harmful side effects. See a PDR (Physician's Desk Reference) for potential hazards of the drugs you are now taking.

2. **Smoking** — this drug causes cancer, birth defects, infertility, hormonal imbalances, heart disease, and other health problems.
3. **Caffeine products** - including colas, coffee, tea, chocolate, and soft drinks. Damage adrenals and sex glands.
4. **Alcohol** — frequent or excessive alcohol consumption **weakens nerves** and weakens sex glands. Robs the body of zinc and B vitamins.
5. **Refined sugars** — lowers energy, increases appetite, and robs the body of B complex, minerals, especially calcium, magnesium and zinc, leaving the sex glands weak and tired.
6. **Processed flour products** — full of refined sugars and devoid of more than 80% of the vitamins and minerals needed for sexual vitality, glandular support, and stamina.
7. **Over-exertion** — studies indicate excessive exercise reduces the amount of estrogen and testosterone in a man's body.
8. **Preservatives and chemical additives** — these products are known to cause cancer, hyperactivity in children, allergies, impotence, infertility, nervous disorders, and other health problems.

9. **Diseases and surgeries** — diabetes, prostate operations, resection of the lower colon or any major abdominal surgery may involve temporary or permanent impotence.
10. **Radiation** — lingering over American cities and received through excessive x-rays can cause both impotence and sterility.
11. **Pesticides** — PCBs, DDT, DES, Pentachlorpherol, Polychlorinated organic chemicals, Hexaclorabengene, Agent Orange, and Bibromochloropane (DBCP).
12. **Synthetic female hormones in meat (see Unsexy Foods Chapter).**

The correction of male impotence and sterility related to physical causes is accomplished by eating the especially **high virility foods** listed in the **OH! YES! Diet** (see chapter). Emphasis should be on pumpkin seeds rich in zinc, Vitamin A, Vitamin E, and unsaturated fatty acids, almonds, sunflower seeds, and sesame seeds (Halva candy) in addition to the whole grains such as buckwheat, millet, and rolled oats. Fertile eggs can be eaten twice a week (soft boiled and poached are the best). Raw yolks pose no cholesterol problems and are easily digested. Yogurt, unsalted butter, olive oil, sesame oil and fish (fin and scale varieties are the best protein-fat combinations).

SUPPLEMENTATION FOR IMPOTENCE AND STERILITY

Vitamin E — d-alpha tocopherols — 400 I.U. three times daily
Wheat Germ Oil — 2 tablespoons a day (only if fresh non-rancid), otherwise virgin olive oil
B-complex — (rice based) — 100mg twice daily
Zinc Chelate (gluconate) — 50mg twice a day
Selenium—50mcg daily
Vitamin C — calcium ascorbate — 2000mg twice daily
Siberian Ginseng — 2 capsules twice daily
Vitamin F — 2 capsules twice a day
Sarsaparilla — 2 capsules twice a day

Many studies indicate that a deficiency of zinc in a diet (common in the Standard American Diet) is associated with impotency, infertility, and prostate disorder. Zinc rich foods and supplements are important in order to increase virility. Whole grains, seeds, and nuts (unsalted and raw), fertile eggs, garlic, and onions are all zinc rich.

DR. TESSLER'S VIRILITY COCKTAIL
(Makes two glasses)

(This is a perfect snack for a busy, tired husband)

1½ glasses apple juice (unsweetened)
2 tbsp. whey powder
2 egg yolks raw (fertile eggs are best)
1 tbsp. wheat germ oil (fresh, non-rancid or olive oil)
1 tbsp. sesame seeds (raw)
2 tbsp. pumpkin seeds (raw)
2 tsp. lecithin granules
1 tsp. bee pollen
1 tbsp. crushed ice

Grind sesame and pumpkin seeds in a seed grinder, then blend all ingredients in a blender. Eat slowly with a spoon or sip with a straw.

WARNING
TIGHT UNDERWEAR COULD MAKE YOU STERILE!

The testicles of a man hang away from his body and are about three degrees cooler than the rest of the body. This insures that sperm can multiply in the millions and keep the man fertile and virile.

Wearing underwear which hold the testicles close to the body (making the sperm too warm) for many hours a day may contribute to sterility. Further studies may show that lower sperm counts in American males over the last fifty years corrolate well with the wearing of tighter men's briefs. **Tapered boxer shorts will permit the testicles to hang loosely.**

PROSTATE PROBLEMS

Prostate troubles have reached epidemic proportions. Medical estimates are that four out of seven men will have prostate problems. The most common prostate disorder is enlargement of the gland. The enlargement can cause blockage of the bladder and can lead to painful urination, inflammation, or infection in the prostate. These symptoms make sexual activity painful or impossible.

The prostate, part of the male sex gland, is normally the size of a chestnut. The gland secretes an alkaline fluid that combines with semen. This alkaline secretion enables the semen to overcome the normal acidity of the vagina. Infertility and unsuccessful impregnation may occur without the secretion of the prostate.

Infection, venereal disease such as gonorrhea, or even tuberculosis of the kidney may impair the function of the prostate.

Abuses of prostate include:

1. Since sexual excitement engorges the penis and prostate with blood, **prolonged excitation without ejaculation** can cause stress resulting in enlargement of the gland.

2. Another abuse of the prostate is caused by the practice of an incomplete sexual act without orgasm.

3. Overuse or abstinence from sexual gratification may cause pressure to build in the prostate gland.

Zinc is very important for general growth and proper development and function of the reproductive organs. The greatest concentrations of zinc are found in the thyroid, pancreas, liver, retina of the eyes, and the **prostate gland. The highest concentration of zinc, in the entire body, is contained in the prostate gland.** Without sufficient zinc levels in the sexual organs, sterility can result and since zinc also helps heal infections, it is **vital** to the healing of prostate infections. Most commercial foods are grown in zinc poor soils and modern methods of processing foods remove the remaining zinc. The potential danger to the prostate from living on processed and refined foods (The Standard American Diet) is obvious. Unprocessed, organic foods are the richest source of zinc. Whole grains, almonds, fertile eggs, sunflower seeds, and pumpkin seeds are especially rich in zinc.

Researchers in Los Angeles treated volunteer victims of enlarged prostate with unsaturated fatty acids, also known as Vitamin F. Thirteen of nineteen patients stopped night urination completely! In all cases the size of the prostate gland was rapidly reduced. Lecithin is a substance which increases the efficiency and effectiveness of Vitamin F as well as other fat soluble vitamins necessary for sexual health (Vitamin A, D, E). According to Dr. Paavo Airola, lecithin is best taken in granular form mixed in juices and sprinkled over cereals, salads, and other foods.

Pumpkin seed oil is an excellent source of zinc and Vitamin F and is very helpful in prostate difficulties.

Another natural product successful in the treatment of prostate disorders is pollen. Swedish studies demonstrate the ability of pollen (Cernilton—Swedish brand of pollen) to relieve acute prostate inflammation. Pollen is discussed in the chapter Aprodisiacs and Natural Hormones.

RECOMMENDATIONS FOR REBUILDING AND MAINTAINING A HEALTHY PROSTATE

1. Moderation is the key to a healthy prostate. Avoid sexual excitement unless a natural conclusion of ejaculation can occur. Prolonged intercourse may lead to functional and structural damage.
2. Eat a diet high in whole grains, seeds, and nuts as a part of the **OH! YES! Diet** outlined under the chapter "Sexy Foods: **OH! YES! Diet.**

3. Avoid smoking, coffee, and alcohol consumption for optimum health of the prostate.
4. Exercise! Walking is the best form of exercise for keeping the prostate in good shape. One to two hours per day is optimum.

SUPPLEMENTATION FOR PROSTATE DISORDERS

Pollen — 2 tsp. per day (locally grown) or 4 tablets.

Zinc — 100mg twice a day first three months, then 50mg twice a day.

Vitamin F (essential fatty acids) — 2 capsules twice a day.

Lecithin granules — 2 tablespoons a day.

Vitamin A — beta carotene — 10,000 units twice a day.

Vitamin C — calcium ascorbate — 2,000mg twice a day for first three months, then 1,000mg twice a day.

Vitamin B-Complex — rice based — 100mg twice a day.

Multi-minerals — natural — 2 tablets a day (take for three months only).

Pumpkin Seed Oil — 2 capsules a day

MALE MENOPAUSE

Authorities are now maintaining that men also experience physiological and psychological changes during their middle years. Men may not lose their reproductive power, but sex drive often diminishes and premature ejaculation is experienced.

Male menopause can begin as early as the late thirties and as late as the fifties. The duration is generally somewhere between ten months and four years.

SYMPTOMS OF MALE MENOPAUSE

Mood swings
Unusual nervousness
Anxiety
Excessive sensitivity

Asocial tendencies
Irritability
Lack of confidence
Increased or decreased sexual interest

The causes of these symptoms may be slowed glandular activity, but even though a man is in his sixties, he can have the sexual activity he did in his twenties. **The fact that so many men are impotent in America is not because they are old but because they are unhealthy.** Studies indicate that a decline in sexual activity of the older male is often the result of a general decline in his physiological capacity. Exercise also invigorates a man, and many men over forty are too sedentary. (See chapter on exercise.)

Alcohol also plays a debilitating role in man's sex drive. **Sexual energy is sparked by excess energy, and a man who eats devitalized foods, smokes, drinks, sleeps poorly, exercises infrequently, and over works can expect to have a shortage, not an excess, of energy.**

SUPPLEMENTATION FOR MALE MENOPAUSE

Vitamin C — calcium ascorbate — 2000mg twice a day
Vitamin E — alpha tocopherols — 400 I.U. twice a day
Garlic (Kyolic Brand) — 2 tablets twice daily
Zinc Chelate — 50mg twice a day
Siberian Ginseng — 2 capsules in the morning
Pollen — 1 teaspoon twice daily
B-Complex — 50mg twice daily (rice based)
Vitamin A — beta carotene — 10,000 I.U. twice daily
Sarsparilla — 2 capsules twice a day

Eat plenty of almonds, olive oil, and pumpkin seeds for increased sexual libido. The **OH! YES! Diet** described in this book is vital to increase energy levels which in turn increase sexual energy levels.

12

Bliss, Blockers and Bloopers

*"The road to ruin is always in good
repair; the travellers pay the expense
of it."*

—W. G. Benham

PREGNANCY

There are more than 250,000 children born with birth
defects every year in the United States and some of these
are linked to smoking and alcohol. Many years of research
may be required before statistical data will establish that
birth defects are caused also by chemicals, additives, per-
servatives, pesticides, herbicides, fungicides, refined sugar,
and poor quality foods. The number of babies born with
physical and mental defects continue to increase. One in ten
newborn babies suffers from some defect.

In addition to an alarming number of birth defects each
year, there are over 400,000 miscarriages annually.

Medical science spends billions of dollars in research to
develop better treatment and care of retarded and deformed
babies and the drug industry spends millions on testing and
developing new miracle drugs for these unfortunates, but
little scientific study or money is spent on how to prevent all
this suffering.

**THE NUMBER ONE FACTOR TO PRODUCE HEALTHY
BABIES IS TO START WITH HEALTHY PARENTS.**

At least a year before conception, both future parents

should make every effort to build optimum health. Here are a few suggestions.

1. Eat the Optimum Health for Youth, Energy, and Sex Diet (OH! YES!).
2. Exercise regularly (at least ½ hour, five days a week). Plenty of Exercise!
3. Take supplements mentioned in *Sex, Nutrition and You* or *Lazy's Person's Guide to Better Nutrition* or *EveryWoman's Book.*
4. Get as much fresh, pure air as possible. Oxygen is more important than food.
5. Drink plenty of pure, bottled water (read *Lazy Person's Guide* for more information on water).
6. Get plenty of sunshine (preferably before 10:00 a.m. or after 4:00 p.m.)
7. Get plenty of sleep, rest and relaxation.

A fetus lives from the nourishment of a mother's body; **make sure mother-to-be that you are well nourished.** Read *Everywoman's Book* by Dr. Paavo Airola, in order to be adequately informed about the important subjects of pre-pregnancy, pregnancy, postpregnancy and lactation. Unhealthy **living habits** of the parents-to-be will increase the chances of a child being born deformed or retarded.

WARNING TO MOTHERS

Aspartame, commonly known as NutraSweet, is approximately 180 times sweeter than sugar and has very few calories. Aspartame is composed of two amino acids, phenylalanine and aspartic acid. With heat and time, aspartame breaks down into methyl alcohol or wood alcohol. Methyl alcohol is a well-known poison. **Ninety-five percent of aspartame becomes formaldehyde in the body, a cancer-producing agent.** Artificial sweeteners, such as cyclamates and sacchrin, have been banned because of the cancers they caused in laboratory animals. We do not know what a "safe level" of methyl alcohol is, or if small amounts of this toxic substance ingested over many years will produce cancers in humans. Other critics remind us of studies indicating that phenylalanine could impair brain development in fetuses of women who are carriers of PKU (phenylketonuria), an inherited metabolic disease. Since most pregnant women are not likely to know whether they are carriers of PKU, critics recommend that all pregnant women avoid using aspartame. The other amino acid, aspartic acid, is absorbed quickly by the brain, and tests on laboratory animals suggest that high quantities of this amino acid also causes brain damage. Common Cause, a Washington, D.C. based consumer group, is challenging the approval of NutraSweet (aspartame) by the Food and Drug Administration. The author agrees with Common Cause that evidence supporting aspartame's safety to public health is inconclusive for F.D.A. approval.

THERE STILL IS NO SAFE ARTIFICIAL SWEETENER AVAILABLE.

CONTRACEPTION

In this century, we have seen two major campaigns to liberate a bodily pleasure from its biological consequences:

1. **To let us have sex without having babies**
2. **To give us a sweet taste without calories**

On the whole, birth control has worked better than girth control.

Contraceptive technology has made us free to enjoy sex without its consequences, yet at what price?

ORAL CONTRACEPTIVES
(99.6% effective)

The pill is a dangerous means of controlling birth rates, even if it has gotten a clean bill of health recently. **The pill** places the body of a woman into a hormonal state similar to a **pregnant woman. This is fine for nine months, but not five, eight or ten years!** Refer to Oral Contraception and P.M.S. in the Women Only chapter for information that makes oral contraception not healthy or advisable.

INTERUTERINE DEVICES (I.U.D.)
(97-99% effective)

The Delcon Shield has been removed from the market because of many law suits against the company for various health reasons. The manufacturers of other I.U.D.'s are so frightened of law suits that many are only producing enough I.U.D.'s for replacement of those women already using one. This device is not safe, healthy or suggested by this author. Public opinion seems to be in agreement with I.U.D.'s lack of safety.

WARNING

Women using the Copper-7 IUD may elevate copper levels which could in turn create zinc deficiencies and hormonal imbalances. None of the IUD's currently on the market are recommended for birth control.

DIAPHRAGM
(93% effective)

This technique has been used for several decades and is proven quite safe for a woman's health. If fitted properly by your doctor and used properly, the diaphragm is an excellent birth control method. The author recommends this device since its safety is high and health risks are low.

CERVICAL CAP
(93% effective)

Studies are still going on regarding the safety of this device. It may prove to be more unsafe than the recent IUD scandal. The cervical cap may produce more infections than the IUD. It is not recommended.

SPONGE
(93% effective)

The sponge seems to be safe and effective birth control if used properly. Usually a sponge is left in the vagina for 24 hours, removed, and then discarded.

FOAM, SPERMICIDAL JELLIES, CREAMS, SUPPOSITORIES, AND TABLETS
(78% effective)

No research has been done to determine the long-range effects of toxic and irritating chemicals in spermicides and jellies to the genital tissues. These toxic chemicals could be absorbed into the mucus membranes of the vagina and perhaps poison other parts of the body. Although there is no apparent danger with these chemicals, more research needs to be done. A possibility but proceed with caution and discontinue if irritation develops.

CONDOMS
(83-96% effective)

In one of the "Rocky" movies, Sylvester Stallone is told by a friend to invest his earnings in condos. Stallone thinks a moment and says, "I never use them." I feel that contraception is at **least fifty** percent the man's responsibility and when used properly, good quality condoms are 83-96% effective. They present no health danger to either the man or the woman. Condoms are the only contraceptive that gives good protection against venereal disease as do contraceptive creams.

Condoms have been used for centuries and with the new technology in condoms, animal skins as well as finer rubber materials make them a natural birth control method. The old technology made wearing condoms during intercourse as attractive as using rubber gloves to pick your nose. Today condoms are of high quality and comfortable. The non-lubricated brands are best since they have no questionable chemicals (pre-lubricated kinds do!).

A man who is man enough to use a condom prevents his wife from being subjected to the risks of cancer, heart disease, infections, and hormonal imbalances caused by oral contraceptives and IUD's. Such a man truly loves and cares for his wife. This method is highly recommended.

VOLUNTARY STERILIZATION

Over two million Americans are sterilized each year. This figure doesn't include hysterectomies. Approximately half of those sterilizations were men, **vasectomies**, and the other half were women, **tubal ligations.**

VASECTOMY

Dr. Gordon A. Kinson, Ph.D., professor of Physiology, Faculty of Medicine, University of Ottawa, completed a study on group rats who received vasectomies. Testosterone levels in testicular-vein blood was reduced to only ten percent. Levels androstenedione were reduced to 60 percent of normal.

If this pattern is true in men as well as rats, vasectomies may mean early decline in sexual desire based upon adrogen lack.

Many men develop allergies to their own sperm, as it is reabsorbed into their systems. This operation alters the immune system in order to attempt to destroy unwanted sperm.

There is also a marked atrophy of the testes from vasectomized rats. Vasectomy appears to amount to a premature aging of the testes. The prostate gland in these rats was significantly reduced in size.

Fatty tissue seemed to grow, equally in the liver area of the vasectomized rats. Certain male hormones needed by the liver to metabolize fat were diminished in the rats.

Vasectomies are too new to assess the possible long-term side effects; however, we can say with some assurance that (1) male hormone levels decrease, (2) the sexual libido decreases and (3) accumulation of fat in the liver occurs. This surgical procedure interfers with the glandular system's normal functioning and leaves the prostate shrunken and malfunctioning.

Symptoms tend to appear in males 7-12 years after the initial operation. Asthmatic symptoms, shortness of breath, tightening of the chest, panic, and feelings of smothering, poor coordination, dizziness and blurred vision are other common symptoms.

A report to the American Fertility Society showed that vasectomized macara fasiculan's monkeys had twice as much atherosclerosis as unvasectomized monkeys. The amount of cholesterol was significantly higher in all major arteries.

This unnatural surgical operation is not recommended for those who want to maintain optimum sexual health, since vasectomies lower male sexual hormones and desires.

TUBAL LIGATION

This surgical operation is too new to discern the long-range effects. Symptoms of tiredness, diminished sex drive, water retention, weight gain, and hormonal imbalances occur two or more years after the operation.

This is not a healthy birth control method since it leaves a woman with sudden fatigue, weight gain, and lowered immunity.

TOTAL FERTILITY AWARENESS METHOD

This form of birth control has been around many centuries and is commonly referred to as the rhythm or calendar method. This method is based on the accurate fact that there are only certain days of the month when a woman can conceive. A few days before ovulation and three days after when conception can occur. The best and safest way to determine the correct cycle is to combine three different methods: (1) calendar method, (2) basal body temperature method and (3) cervical mucus, according to Dr. Paavo Airola, *Everywoman's Book.* Planned Parenthood in your city has precise directions for each of these methods as does Dr. Airola's book.

SEXUALLY TRANSMITTED DISEASES

GONORRHEA

Gonorrhea is the most common bacterial sexual infection of adults. Most gonorrhea infections are symptom free (none). Because this infection has a short incubation period, it spreads rapidly.

Gonorrhea infects the mucus-producing membranes of the cervix and urethra. This infection is treated with antibiotics—particularly penicillin. Women, after taking antibiotics, may develop a vaginal yeast infection called candidians. Gonococci bacteria can enter the reproductive organs of men or women, causing permanent damage such as sterility. Gonorrhea can also cause blindness, eye infections, and arthritis in the newborn. In the late 1950s, 300,000 units of penicillin would cure gonorrhea, but today even doses of five million units don't affect some strains of the bacteria.

LOCAL SYMPTOMS
(if any)

MEN	WOMEN	BOTH
urethra	**cervix**	**anus**
discharge of pus from penis	thick yellowish discharge from vagina	burnings or itching rectum
burning on urination	cervical inflammation and/or bumbs on cervix (granular erosions)	mucusy stools or bloody/pus discharge (both rarely)
cloudy urine		

	urethra	**throat**
	burning on urination	mild sore throat
	cloudy urine	severe sore throat (rarely)

	Bartholin's Glands	**eyes**
	swelling, itching, pan	swelling and inflammation
		pus discharge

WHAT CAN HAPPEN TO YOU

MEN	LOCALLY
infection of the prostate and epididymis	damage to sperm ducts
testicular involvement marked by swelling, pain and fever	scarring in urethra that can interfere with urination and fertility
abscesses in urethral glands	
infections under foreskin	

WOMEN

spread to uterus, fallopian tubes and ovaries, leading to PID (pelvic inflammatory disease)

chronic PID, with pain and fever

spread to the peritoneum, the membranous sac covering the abdominal walls and intestines, leading to peritonitis

scarring of fallopian tubes, which can cause sterility and increase the chance of an ectopic (tubal) pregnancy

infections of the joints (arthritis)

heart and liver infections, which may be fatal

meningitis, which may be fatal

abscesses involving vital organs, such as liver

BOTH

damage to cornea

blindness

*Courtesy: *Healthy Sex*

HERPES SIMPLEX
(Type 2)

There are approximately twenty million cases of genital herpes (one out of five American adults) and another half million new cases each year. Of those that contract the virus, about half have a single occurrence or very rare reoccurrence. Only ten percent of those with herpes have multiple reoccurrences. Although herpes is incurable, so are cold sores (Herpes Simplex Type 1)! Both need to run their infectious cycles. Millions of people infected with Herpes Simplex never transmitted the disease to their sex partner. So, if you have it, remain calm. Physical or emotional stress seems to bring back a reoccurrence of the disease. Anything which compromises a person's resistance could reactivate the virus. Sunburn, other infections, drugs, and stress can encourage its return. Herpes virus lives in nerve cells of the brain and spinal cord, causing symptoms **only** when it is activated.

Taking Lysine (1000mg three times a day) while symptoms are present speeds herpes remission. Take 500mg of Lysine regularly between episodes.

SOLUTION

Both gonorrhea and herpes simplex are infections, either viral or bacterial. Lowered resistance to infection increases a person's chances of contracting not only venereal diseases but many other diseases. Increasing the resistance or immunity of the body will permit the natural antibodies to fight any infection until victory over such viruses. **The same endocrine glands that produce the many sexual hormones also produce antibodies which fight infection and heal wounds.**

Essentially only the natural ability of our immune system to defend itself determines whether illness takes hold. The body, in the final analysis, **must be the hero.**

Much fear and vast sums of money are being spent toward AIDS (Acquired Immune Deficiency Syndrome), another sexually transmitted disease. Instead of discovering vaccines and drugs to combat an ever-increasing range of viruses, germs and bacteria, the primary need is to **strengthen** the immune system itself. The OH! YES! diet, eaten for generations by people almost totally free of diseases that plague the West, **will** assist in building our precious immunological system.

Nature has equipped us with a fabulous defense system. This system protects us from harmful, "foreign" invaders. It is a gift we inherit at birth, but a prized possession we must maintain. Good nutrition, regular exercise, vitamin and mineral supplementation, proper sleep, and reduced stress are vital in order to assure a strong immunological army to fight an internal battle for us.

When the immune system or endocrine gland depletes, colds, flus, allergies, candida, hypoglycemia, sexually transmitted diseases, and degenerative diseases are the result.

The supplements mentioned in the Vitamin and Mineral Chapter are all helpful to the immune system. A supplement program and diet for allergies is well covered in *Lazy Person's Guide to Better Nutrition*. Certain supplements build up the resistance of the body coupled with the OH! YES! diet. Other foods can destroy the immune system. **RESISTANCE IS THE KEY TO PROTECT YOUSELF FROM INFECTIONS AND DISEASES OF ALL TYPES.**

CANDIDA

These organisms **normally** live throughout the body, including mouth, intestines and vagina. They present no problems **unless** antibiotics are taken. Antibiotics destroy not only harmful viruses and bacteria, but the beneficial bacteria and antibodies, too. These beneficial bacteria would keep the candida under control if not killed off by these antibiotics. Remember **anti** means **against** and **biotics** means **life,** so antibiotics are against life! The answer to candida sufferers is to **build up** the **immune system** or in other words, the endocrine gland system. Women with vaginal yeast infections increase the candida colonies by wearing panty hose, tight pants, and synthetic underwear. Tight, cramped and a warm environment in which yeast can grow.

To relieve uncomfortable yeast infections put a clove of fresh garlic in the vagina overnight for a few days. The vagina may become swollen, but yeast and swelling will leave quickly. Stay away from antibiotics as much as possible. Instead, use this natural formula to assist with the healing process of your body.

TAKE FOR THREE DAYS ONLY

Vitamin C (ascorbate) — 2,000mg three times a day
Calcium Chelate — 1,000mg twice a day
Vitamin A (beta carotene) — 50,000 units twice a day
Gold Seal **Root** — 2 capsules twice a day

CONCLUSION

The National Cancer Institute, American Cancer Society, and American Heart Association recommend that Americans limit fats, salt, and refined sugar in their diet and increase complex carbohydrates, fish, and poultry (low in fat), fruits (rich in A and C) and vegetables (rich in A and C).

These agencies are convinced, due to the overwhelming evidence, that a poor diet is a **primary cause** of cancer, diabetes and heart disease. Further scientific investigation in the next few years will continue to reveal that sexual dysfunction in its various forms is also related to dietary ignorance.

These same agencies are suggesting that certain natural foods added to the diet can **protect** and **prevent** the onset of these degenerative diseases. *Sex, Nutrition and You* has presented information which can correct or maintain a healthy sex life by building optimum health. The recommendations contained in these pages are based not on opinion but on history. The history of healthy, strong and sexually active people around the world. It is a history of people living wholesome and active lives. The foods these people have used for centuries to promote good health which have permitted long, productive life spans, is contained within the covers of this work. The natural herbal hormones and sexually exciting foods (aphrodisiacs), as well as the supplements needed to support the energy requirements of your sex glands and hormones has also been given to you.

A good lover must be a good eater. He or she must be aware of the food which contribute to hormonal health and sexual activity. Without the raw materials (vitamins and minerals) derived from the OH! YES! diet, the entire body becomes vulnerable to sickness and disease. Sexual disease and sexual dysfunction are part of the total range of degeneration so epidemic in the United States.

May this book, *Sex, Nutrition, and You,* convince, inspire and stimulate you to seek Optimum Health for Youth, Energy and Sex. Nutritional knowledge is unlike most other kinds of knowledge; it must be lived to be appreciated. **Nutrition is a process, not an end.**

—Gordon S. Tessler, Ph.D.

Dear Dr. Tessler,

Thank you. . . .

_____

Your name

Better Health Publishers
3368 Governor Drive
Suite F-224
San Diego, CA 92122

References

Hamilton, Eva May Nannelley, *Nutrition, Concepts and Controversies,* St. Paul, Minnesota, West Publishing Co., 1982. One of the finest text books on nutrition ever written for the college level student.

Nilsson, Tennort, *Behold Man*, Boston, Massachusetts, Little, Brown, Company, 1974. Enlarged photographs, in color, of the various organs, tissues and glands of the human body along with a text of their functions.

Grey, Henry, *Grey's Anatomy*, New York, Bounty Books, 1977 edition. This book is the queen of the basic sciences and used by many medical schools in the field of human biology.

Pfeiffer, Ph.D., M.D., *Mental and Elemental Nutrients,* New Canoon, Connecticut, Keats Publishing Co., 1975. A clinical nutrition book covering research on most vitamins, minerals, and microminerals and their effect in the human body.

Airola, Paavo, *Everywoman's Book*, Phoenix, Arizona, Health Plus Publishers, 1979. After reading this complete self-help book, the woman who is interested in health can be her own family doctor most of the time.

Kilham, Christopher Scott, *Stalking the Wild Organism*, San Diego, California, ACS Publications, 1984. A book about how to achieve sexual well-being through nutrition and exercise.

Jensen, Bernard, Ph.D., *The Chemistry of Man,* Escondido, California. Self-published, 1983. A text book of chemical elements and their need in correctional nutrition for prevention and reversal of disease.

Cheraskin, E., M.D., *Diet and Disease*, Connecticut, Keats Publishing, Inc., 1968. Medical proof of the life and death relationship between degenerative diseases and their prevention through proper nutrition.

Jeans, Helen, *Grains, Nuts, and Seeds.* Great Britain, Weatherly Woolnorgh Ltd., 1978. A historical and nutritional book of grains, seeds, and nuts, elaborating the nutritional bounty contained in these storehouses of natural goodness.

Bieler, Henry G., M.D., *Food Is Your Best Medicine,* New York, Vintage Books, 1973. A classic in the nutrition literature discussing how proper nutrition cures endocrine imbalances.

Meyer, Clarence, *Fifty Years of the Herbalist Almanac,* Glenwood, Illinois, Meyer Books, 1977. A text book outlining the medicinal and therapeutic uses of plants.

Santillo, Hembart, B.S., *Natural Healing With Herbs*, Prescott Valley, Arizona, Hohm Press, 1984. A complete manual for the use of herbs for every dimension of life.

Deeton, William T., *Biological Science*, Cornell University, New York, W.W. Norton and Company, 1972. A biological text book of very readable quality for the college level student.

Seaman, Barbara and Gideon, M.D., *Women and the Crisis in Sex Hormones,* New York, Bantana Books, 1979. A complete guide to all aspects of female sexual functions written by the foremost cynicologists in the field.

Bumgarner, Marlene Anne, *The Book of whole Grains,* New York, St. Martin's Press, 1976. An outstanding recipe book outlining the discovery and contribution of whole grains in the human body.

Airola, Paavo, *How To Get Well*, Phoenix, Arizona, Health Plus Publishers, 1974. A nutritional self-help book outlining over sixty different ailments and the nutrition diet and supplements for each.

Williams, Roger J., M.D., *The Prevention of Alcoholism Through Nutrition,* New York, Bantam Books, 1981. This book presents in layman's terms information on nutrition to prevent alcoholism and many alcohol related problems from developing.

Airola, Paavo, Ph.D., *Rejuvenation Secrets from Around the World,* Phoenix, Arizona, Health Plus Publishers, 1981. A book that shares the nutritional secrets of health cultures from all over the world.

Hunter, Beatrice Trum, *Additives Book*, Connecticut, Keats Publishing, Inc., 1980. This book informs all of us about the hazards to human health from chemicals in our foods.

Lumiere, Richard, M.D., *Healthy Sex and Keeping It That Way,* New York, Simon and Schuster, 1983. A complete guide to sexual infections and how to treat them medically.

Christopher, John R., *School of Natural Healing,* Provo, Utah, Bi-World Publishers, 1979. A reference volume on natural herbs for the teacher, student, and herbal practitioner.

Nutrition Almanac, Nutrition Research, Inc., New York, McGraw-Hill Book Company, 1979. A complete reference book to nutrients, nutrition and their application in human nutrition.

Robertson, Laurel, *Laurel's Kitchen,* New York, Bantam Books, 1976. Excellent natural cookbook for beans and whole grains.

Lark, Susan M., M.D., *The Premenstrual Syndrome Self-Help Book,* Los Altos, California, PMS Self-Help Center, 1984. Excellent help for women who wish to heal PMS problems through nutritional means.

Wood, Lawrence, M.D., *Your Thyroid*, Boston, Massachusetts, Houghton Mifflin, 1985. This book explains how the third gland effects weight gain and loss, hormonal difficulties and even nervous disorders.

Cook, Cynthia, M.D., *"It's Time to Take Male Infertility Seriously,"* Ms. Magazine, March 1981.

READING LIST

Dr. Airola's Books — Health Plus Publishing, P.O. Box 22001, Phoenix, Arizona 85028.

1. Every Woman's Book
2. How To Get Well
3. Are You Confused?
4. Garlic
5. How To Keep Slim, Healthy & Young Through Juice Fasting
6. Rejuvenation Secrets From Around The World
7. Hypoglycemia — A Better Approach

Dr. Jensen's Books — Bernard Jensen Publishing, Route 1, Box 52, Escondido, California 92025.

1. Nature Has A Remedy
2. You Can Master Disease
3. The Chemistry Of Man
4. World Keys to Health and Long Life
5. Tissue Cleansing Through Bowel Movement

COOKBOOKS

The Book of Whole Grains, Marlene Anne Bumgarner, St. Martin's Press, 175 Fifth Avenue, New York, N.Y. 10010.

The Garlic Lover's Cookbook, Gilroy Garlic Festival Association, P.O. Box 2311, Gilroy, California 95021.

Airola Diet and Cookbook, Dr. Paavo Airola, Health Plus Publishers, 2218 East Magnolia, Phoenix, Arizona 85034.

GOVERNMENT PUBLICATIONS

Amino Acid Content of Foods, Home Economics Research Report No. 4, U.S. Department of Agriculture, 1968.

Composition of Foods, Agricultural Handbook No. 8, Agricultural Research Service, U.S. Department of Agriculture, 1963.

Dietary Goals for the United States, Select Committee on Nutrition and Human Needs, U.S. Senate, U.S. Printing Office, 1977.

Nutrition Action, Center for Science in the Public Interest, 1501 16th Street NW, Washington, D.C. 20036.

Index

sweeteners in foods and
beverages, 66-69
average consumption, 70
sugar as thief, 72-73
substitutes, 139

men's golden plus pak, 58
women's golden plus pak,
59
Synthetic Hormones in Meat,
83-85

S

Salt, 73-75
substitutes, 139
Seeds, 102-107, 126
pumpkin, 121
sesame, 121-122
sunflower, 122-123
Sexually Transmitted Diseases,
222-226
Gonorrhea, 222-224
Herpes Simplex, 224-225
Snacks, 130-131
Sterility, 207-210
Substitution for Unsexy Foods,
131-135
Supplementation
reasons to take, 25-26
general directions, 56
men's staying power pak,
57
women's staying power
pak, 58

T

Tubal Ligation, 221-222

V

Vasectomy, 220-221
Vegetables, 126
Vitamins
Vitamin A, 44-46
Vitamin B, 46-48
Vitamin C, 48-51
Vitamin D, 51-53
Vitamin E, 53-55
Vitamin F, 55-56
Voluntary Sterilization,
220-222

W

Water, 135
Well-Balanced Diet, 25-26,
61-65

NOTES: